Remarriage

and
God's Renewing Grace

A Positive Biblical Ethic
for Divorced Christians

Dwight Hervey Small

BAKER BOOK HOUSE
Grand Rapids, Michigan 49506

Copyright 1986 by
Baker Book House Company

Library of Congress
Card Catalog Number: 86–70161

ISBN 0-8010-8264-1

Printed in the United States of America

To pastors and counselors, who daily encounter the pain and devastation of divorce together with the hope of healing and normalcy in remarriage, this study reinforces the truth that God does not minister through inflexible, prohibitive law but in forgiving, renewing grace.

To divorced Christians, some now remarried, who have suffered most from legalistic Bible teaching, strictures of fellow Christians, and the indignity of non-accepting churches, this study carries a reassuring message—*There is a new wind blowing!*

Contents

Foreword

Today 45 percent of all first marriages end in divorce!

Today 55 percent of all second marriages end in divorce!

The increasing incidence of divorce in our society is appalling. Perhaps what is even worse is the way the church in the past has dealt with those who have traveled the rocky road through divorce country. Divorced persons have been shunned, criticized, and condemned and also excluded from many things in church life.

In early 1975 I became aware of the ill treatment of those who were struggling through a divorce. That awareness prompted me to offer a workshop/seminar for those whose lives were shattered by divorce. I believe God is in the renewal, reclamation, recovery, and forgiveness business. I also believe that his grace initiates new beginnings in the lives of battered and scarred Christians.

In this much-needed and long-awaited book Dwight Small addresses the biblical issues of divorce and remarriage from the practical and theological perspective. He answers the one question that I have been asked hundreds of times in my seminars: "Can a divorced Christian remarry and still be in the will and service of God?" With clarity and loving insight, Small guides the reader through biblical teachings on divorce and remarriage. He also aptly addresses the teachings on divorce espoused by legalists.

This gentle book by Dwight Small meets the need for a positive biblical resource on the issues of divorce and remarriage. It should be read by every caring Christian.

Jim Smoke
Orange, California

Introduction

This book is a study of biblical teaching as it concerns Christians now divorced, divorced and remarried, or facing this possibility. To the author's knowledge, it is quite unlike any study presently available, in its approach to biblical ethics as well as in its positive affirmations. It moves beyond merely ascertaining the meaning of individual Bible texts and stringing them together in order to arrive at an ethic to fit all cases alike. Correct exposition of all relevant Scripture is, of course, essential. Here God alone speaks authoritatively, providing the basis for Christian social ethics. Indeed, any social ethic worthy of Christian consideration must first pay meticulous attention to the statement and probable meaning of Scripture. But at this point do we then simply sum up the biblical statements, making direct and universal application to all divorce and remarriage regardless of circumstances? Not at all. We have the parallel task of establishing a theological basis for ethics, asking several questions: What is the ruling ethic of the New Covenant founded upon Christ's death and resurrection? Is it a new law, with penalties for all who fail? Or does it set forth God's ideal, with redemptive provisions for broken relationships, including failed marriages? Does forgiving, renewing grace apply only to restoration of first marriages or to remarriages as well? These are the questions with which we must wrestle. Quite simply, the author's approach develops around this thesis: *The ruling ethic of the New Covenant is the forgiving, renewing grace of God in Christ. Whenever marriage failure is unresolvable— irreversibly so—then God's purpose, although never compromised, is mediated by grace. Renewing grace carries the possibility of positive new beginnings, not negative prohibitions. Thus, prohibitive legalism is ruled out by grace.*

It is correct to surmise that in the pages that follow the author will project his own personal bias with reference to the right of remarriage. This bias arises out of nearly forty years of ministry to divorced Christians, and the bias has changed radically over the years. Change has consistently been in the direction of disciplined freedom in God's grace and a more positive approach to the practice of remarriage. I should add that it is a more responsible one as well.

Having taught the marriage courses at Westmont College for some years, emphasizing the permanency of marriage in God's unchanging purpose, it seemed necessary at last to balance this fundamental emphasis with an honest, compassionate look at divorce and remarriage apart from traditional legalism. Inevitably this required a measure of response to evangelical hard-liners whose views, widely taught in our day, are difficult for the average Christian to assess without professional help. These teachings tend to be predominantly negative and intimidating, rarely caring and helpful. The better word is "devastating."

Perhaps we all struggle with the tendency to look for simple, universal solutions to complex problems. Should we seek one rule to cover the vast diversity of divorce cases? Traditionally we have tended to say, "one rule only." But not today. All divorces do not spring from the same causes, bear the same characteristics, concern people with the same background or maturity, or produce the same consequences for individuals or families. So to treat all divorces by the same rule is a mistake. However much we might wish it, no single rule applies to all cases; only a very restricted view of Scripture makes it seem so. Furthermore, in attempting to make a single rule apply universally, we reduce the Bible to an inflexible code book, making it offer uniform solutions to problems that, although very similar in some respects, are not exactly alike. Why do we do this? From some strong need within ourselves to always have universal answers— forcing Scripture to speak to situations where in fact it does not? Or making it say what we believe it ought to say? Do we feel more comfortable sidestepping tough, intricate questions like divorce and remarriage, trusting in a solve-it-with-a-single-biblical-prescription approach? A comfortable cop-out indeed!

Granted, there are tempting benefits to be gained from this method. It is certainly safer to have ready-made solutions we can pull out and apply, whatever the situation and whenever it arises. It gives the appearance of our being knowledgeable, unshakably certain of our answers. When we speak with lofty ministerial authority, people can rest assured as to just where we stand. We are not so likely to be charged with dealing in ambiguities or dodging issues that demand a "Thus saith the Lord" answer. We know that this is what many people want.

Now, of course, it is well and good whenever we can legitimately pronounce, "Thus said the Lord"—indeed it is our clear responsibility to do so. But we dare not make this the easy way around difficult problems where differences must be identified and principles diversely and appropriately applied. However much we might wish Scripture to bear full responsibility for decisions *we* must make, we cannot exonerate ourselves in this way. We simply have to wrestle with the social complexities that demand our personal discretion, even though we may only partially comprehend the magnitude of all that is involved. God does not relieve us of this responsibility.

Scripture provides us with moral principles and perspectives sufficient for clear guidance. While it is always easier when we have scriptural examples to light the way, it is not so easy when we must attempt to make specific applications of the more general ethic of redemptive grace.

It becomes increasingly clear why we look in vain for the New Testament to supply detailed codes of conduct to fit every situation. Jewish scribes attempted this in their time and failed. It is not the New Testament pattern. Nor does the New Testament concern itself with the relative merits of this particular case or that. Scripture does not, as it were, "pick up the loose ends." How often in decision making we are left to move with the guidance of God's Word and Spirit along a course of responsible freedom under the lordship of Jesus Christ. We look to the dynamic ministry of the Holy Spirit to bring additional insight, enabling us to apply Scripture properly. So often in the midst of a moral dilemma, even with Bible in hand, we can do no better than pray, "O God, by Your Spirit grant me wisdom and guidance in this baffling matter." It is then that Word and Spirit meet with our spirit to give us understanding and guidance.

Sometimes all Scripture provides is a rudimentary basis for an ethical decision. By "rudimentary" we refer to the manner in which the gospel was put into practice in the circumstances of the apostolic period, in certain given situations. The apostles were given initial insight to begin working out the principles of kingdom ethics in the local situations encountered in the course of their ministry. The New Testament writers did not attempt to settle every ethical issue in advance of its emergence in history and cultural development. They were not, and could not be, knowledgeable of all possible situations as they might arise in future centuries of the church's life. Nor did God by His Spirit choose to illumine their minds so they could know; this was not His intent. What He did give them, and what they faithfully transmitted to future generations, were some absolutes of kingdom righteousness. But in a fallen world and in an imperfect, immature, and sometimes failing church, these absolutes, while ever remaining the standard, must of necessity be applied in a provisional manner because of man's weakness and sinfulness. God in grace accommodates His righteous demands to the limitations of a people redeemed yet sometimes failing to live out those Christian life demands.

The highest measure of Christian conduct is the measure of God's character revealed in Jesus Christ. We must be absolutely sure that the solution to social problems such as divorce and remarriage will always be in full conformity with the character of God. So we need a clear vision of the divine character every bit as much as we need the statement of moral principles. In the biblical disclosure of God's character is included His unconditional love, operating through forgiving and renewing grace. These divine attributes invariably stand over against any ethic built on prohibitive, inflexible legalism.

Inasmuch as this book has to do with the remarriage of divorced Christians, the lives of men and women are at stake, yes, and of their children also. The author does not wish his more "open" position to be regarded with finality or necessarily as being of greater merit than that of other writers, but only that special attention be given to the thesis that the ruling ethic of the New Covenant in Christ is that of redeeming, renewing grace—grace that not only forgives failure and sin but seeks renewal of all normal, God-ordained avenues of full family life. Families are not to be left in a broken condition.

I like what someone said recently—that spiritual maturity is the confidence we place in fellow Christians, which enables us to walk arm in arm when we cannot see eye to eye. We are seeking to deal sensitively with a subject around which there is continued debate. In the love of Jesus you are invited to consider a viewpoint that may not be yours as you begin this study, and may not be yours when you have completed it. But as earnest fellow seekers of God's truth and will, as those who together want God's Word to speak clearly and compellingly, may we walk arm in arm even though we do not see eye to eye! But if we do see eye to eye, if we do share the same light, then perhaps God is doing a renewing work in which we both shall share the benefits. Truly, this would be our fondest hope!

Note: For further amplification of the author's methodology, see Appendix D.

PART ONE

The Broader Biblical Understanding of Marriage, Divorce, and Remarriage

1

New Wind Blowing

Pastor, have I the right to remarry? It's been nearly four years now since John decided he wanted out. I've been seeing a fine Christian widower, and the children feel as I do that we could reestablish a Christian family and normalize our lives again. Pastor, have I a right to remarry?

In one form or another that question repeats itself daily. Perhaps no more controversial subject haunts the church than that of divorce and remarriage. To write on the subject is to place oneself in the midst of a highly emotionalized and dogmatically controverted debate. For today it is not simply a matter of academic interest; it touches the lives of countless evangelical Christians presently either divorced and remarried, or divorced and alone—alone with children, most likely.

Redemptive Realism

In one way or another, the church has seen to it that the divorced cannot forget their peculiar status. To be divorced and unattached is to be an anomaly in the fellowship, a fifth wheel consigned to a most difficult and untenable position. To be divorced and now remarried is only less difficult because it is less known. But for those the stigma and strictures are all around and readily felt. Sadly, Christians tend to project their own hidden failures upon others whose failures are more conspicuous. We look for scapegoats upon whom we can lay our own guilts. The divorced are ready-made targets. We seem to look better in our own eyes when we can look down upon another person we can point to as being less successful than we are. The divorced, even if not rejected in overt ways, are often treated as second-class citizens in the kingdom of God. Pastors victimized by divorce commonly find themselves no longer acceptable in the ministry. Thankfully, this is changing dramatically in many church organizations. More frequently, it is lay people who discover themselves no longer considered worthy to serve as church officers or Sunday-school teachers. Such persons are no longer "proper Christian models." Regardless of the conditions surrounding the marital breakup, the message is tacitly communicated that divorce must bear a moral stigma. This inevitably leads to some form of social ostracism, be it ever so subtle.

Strange, but one can be forgiven nearly any other failure known to human life and be restored to a place of service in the church—confession and penitence are all that are required. But it seems that to be divorced and remarried is to have committed unpardonable sin for which there is no restoration to service for Christ in the church. A respected Christian leader, recently the victim of divorce, said she learned only too quickly that the church is the only army that shoots its own wounded. Can this be true?

This book is a protest to all forms of non-acceptance and demeaning attitudes expressed toward divorced and remarried fellow Christians. It is a call for an end to this kind of injustice and ecclesiastical immorality! Let us cease keeping our divorced the minority most discriminated against in our loving Savior's family! To this end the challenge is to present the case for "redemptive realism"— the far better way!

To contemporary evangelical pastors, divorce has become

a perplexing dilemma by virtue of the growing number of divorced-remarried persons in their congregations, many of whom would qualify as their most committed and gifted Christian men and women. They sense a certain incongruity between the real-life situation and what the church has persistently taught over the years. They are aware of the struggle within denominations and in evangelical circles especially. While the trend is clearly toward a broader view, change does not come easily. Peer pressure in the ministry can be severe. But the question is unavoidable: Do we or do we not have new insights into divorce-and-remarriage ethics, insights developed in the light of today's complex circumstances? Do we not have a greater understanding of scriptural ethics? In other words, does not the modern urgency of the problem and its increasing incidence warrant a deeper look at what God is saying—not in isolated texts alone but in the overall ethic of redemptive grace? Do we not need more than proof-text proscriptions? We must press on to address these critical questions forthrightly.

In the failure of the church to provide a "new word," our divorced-remarried Christian friends frequently turn to secular sources for help in making the difficult transitions they face. The impression is only too easily gained that the world cares more about them than does the church to which they have looked for support. The author is ever grateful for the ministry of those like his friend Jim Smoke, leader in divorce-recovery seminars nationally. Another friend, Charles Cerling, is doing some important writing in this area. (See *For Further Reading* at the close of this book.) If ministry to the divorced is to be effective, their Christian status must first be assured. If pastors view the divorced only as embarrassments within the church—exhibits of failure—they may counsel them toward the end of recovering emotional and spiritual health, but they still hold out no hope that normal family life can be restored or that the Christian community will welcome their full participation. The aura of unspoken judgment preserves a hidden sense that somehow a penalty is being inflicted. According to many divorced people, such suffering at the hands of the church is very great indeed. Where, then, shall they find practical examples of the grace that the church proclaims doctrinally with such fervor? If in this most demanding of intimate relationships no fully redemptive possibility exists, how can such possibilities be expected in other areas where Christian people make irreversible mistakes? Is redemptive realism an all-embracing concept or not?

On a more personal level, this book is designed to bring reassurance to remarried Christians, to say to them that God's redeeming, renewing grace reaches to every condition of life, offering possibilities forever shut off by prohibitive legalism. God enters into our situation to bring forth good, whatever that situation is and however we got there. We can appreciate the emphasis of Lewis Smedes that not all failure is moral failure. True, we are all moral agents responsible for our actions, but at times we are victims as well. We are victims of a culture relentlessly hostile to our Christian values. We are victims of the actions of other people. We are victims of our own fragile natures. Smedes makes the strong point that the church must minister to the divorced as "victims."

May the message of these pages serve to challenge pastors to consider a ministry more in harmony with the principles of grace that dominate New Testament ethics. Granted, guidelines for the church do not establish divorce and remarriage as a personal right, as a biblical option; permission is not based on the orders of creation nor provided for in kingdom law. It is permissible because redemptive grace and the provisional will of God do not preclude it under appropriate circumstances. Although never God's pure intention, divorce and remarriage sometimes come within His provisional will for those facing irreversible marital breakup. It is not that the grace of realized forgiveness suspends God's absolute ethical demand or compromises it in any way. Instead, divine grace transcends all legal judgments in the wake of divorce. Grace is restorative, not punitive, extending even to the sinful disruption of the marital commitment. In plain words, grace extends even to the guilty party.

The "One Flesh" Covenant

Whenever the question of divorce and remarriage is raised in evangelical circles, the answers conventionally fall along three lines. Either "Scripture allows no divorce at all," citing Jesus' words in Mark and Luke as final authority. Or, "Divorce is allowable only in the case of a partner's adultery," citing Jesus' words in Matthew. Here remarriage is allowed by some, not by others. Or, lastly, it is permissible for the reason just given, but also if an unbelieving partner wants it, citing Paul in First Corinthians. Here again, some allow remarriage, others do not. Interpretation divides at more than one juncture.

Surely a problem of this magnitude and with such serious implications for pastoral ministry and life within the church ought to send us back to the presuppositions of our theology, searching every possibility of a broader ethical framework than that we have previously known. Of course, utmost care must be given not to allow the impression that divorce is to be taken lightly, or that no ethical or spiritual consequences need be expected. Indeed, there is no such thing as an "ideal divorce." Every divorce, however justified, further diminishes the social bonds that communities most value. We affirm with Dominic Crossan: "The bond of marriage is privileged in law because it is sacred for life. It confines and protects the family as the primary community of love. The inherent durability of the marital union is necessary for the realization of the basic values of civilized society, and so it has been sustained in all nations by the rule of law." Of even greater importance, marriage as ordained of God in the orders of creation is meant to be indissoluble. Of greater significance than what marriage *does*—its instrumental function—is what marriage *means*. This shall be taken up at length in chapter two.

Suffice it to say here that marriage is a covenant of love

and fidelity, symbolizing the unity of two persons in the total-
ity of their existence. It is established on the model of Christ's
relationship to His church. It is more than the integration of
persons in a common endeavor; it is their unity of mind,
body, spirit. Mutuality and complementarity make the
marital union something more than the mere addition of
two lives; the whole is greater than the sum of its parts. The
couple is so united as to be "one flesh," a biblical expression
signifying their total unity as persons.

By these standards, what is left of marriage when it fails
as a catalyst for a couple's welfare, is no longer a covenant of
love and fidelity? What is marriage if it no longer is a unity
of persons in their totality, a relationship of practiced mutuality? Whenever marriage ceases to exist as God intended
it—whatever other marital characteristics may be present—
what then? When marriage creates loneliness and a sense of
separation, when meaningful communication is no longer
possible, and when the integration of persons has been sup-
planted by disintegration, then what truly defines this as
marriage? Bereft of its essential meaning and purpose,
marriage may witness only that two people continue living
alongside each other, enacting all the marital rituals in a
perfunctory manner. For all practical purposes, the marriage is dead. Then the Christian symbolism of marriage as
a reflection of God's covenant *love for* and *union with* man no
longer has substance. At this point, no formal contractual
recognition in law can make this a true marriage. Divorce
de facto is the true reality; divorce *de jure* awaits only the
formalities of the courts. Long before a formal divorce gives
recognition to the marital dissolution there remains nothing to give meaning to the claim of "what God has joined
together." Two human spirits are already in a state of divorce.

Prohibition of Divorce—Really?

Absolute prohibition of divorce, even prohibition except
for the cause of adultery, no longer commends the adherence
of many responsible Christian leaders today. Quite frankly,

the debate in theological ethics is moving in another direction, away from the question of justifiable cause to the larger question of what God is seeking to do in the lives of those who are caught in the throes of marital conflict and dissolution. This book is a serious call to pastors and counselors to study the new concerns and new biblical approaches. And to those who are divorced, it is a word of encouragement and personal assurance.

Some pastors tend to resist any new or seemingly unconventional approach simply because it is unfamiliar and hence suspect. Others are fearful because of an entrenched bias against all divorce, which characterizes much of the evangelicalism they hold dear. Long-held views tend to become sacrosanct, hence difficult to dislodge. Yet we have only to look at the history of doctrinal development to see progressive change. It is, of course, understandable that any treatment of divorce that appears to make it more acceptable is likely cause for concern, lest it seem to contribute to the breakdown of the family institution in our already-troubled day. But truth always bears the risk of misunderstanding and abuse. Responsible minds must be willing to face every new implication of truth while energetically countering any attempted abuse. Nor can we allow those whose thinking is on the cutting edge, who are looking to God to shed new light from His Word, to be intimidated by those with closed minds and loud voices.

The enigma faced by many thoughtful pastors is that Jesus' words, simply taken by themselves, lay down such a stringent moral judgment as to make God's purpose seem tantamount to an absolute prohibition of all divorce. Even when the death of a marriage proves undeniably final, we tend to deny that reality nonetheless, pretending that since it might have been otherwise, why is it not? The very nature of faith inclines us to believe that nothing is so bad as to be irreversible. Thus we are somewhat preconditioned not to recognize divorce and the permissibility of remarriage. This can cause serious misjudgment, for it contends against the nature of forgiveness and redemptive grace. The notion of a lifelong penalty for dissolution of life's most demanding and fragile relationship seems incongruous with the redemptive character of God. This, too, is a divine standard.

As an example of what follows upon this kind of denial, one of the nation's prominent teachers in the area of youth conflicts repeats to large audiences everywhere, "We must remove the option of divorce." Yes, a noble aspiration with which we could agree—except for one thing: it is a sheer impossibility in this life! What we really need, it seems, is the biblical view of a compassionate God whose forgiving, renewing grace reaches out to all who—in the face of a destructive, irreparable marriage—have found no other way but divorce. *The option we really need to remove is the option of condemnation and unloving rejection!*

Is the Bible a Code Book?

The absolute prohibition of all divorce appeals to those who see the Bible as a code book—a directory of unrelenting rules rather than principles for intended action. This view makes the New Testament ethic little different from the Old Testament ethic based on Mosaic law. That Jesus radicalized Mosaic law in His kingdom ethic seems to some a further confirmation that it is law that underlies all Christian ethics. As we have suggested elsewhere, this is to confuse different periods in which God administers moral principles in different ways. This is not "dispensationalism" but simply the recognition that God acts differently toward His people today than under Mosaic law. *The church age is characterized by forgiving grace instead of condemning law.* Although the church age is characterized, too, by the Holy Spirit's enabling power in the believer's life, perfect fulfillment of kingdom principles necessarily remains incomplete. Forgiving grace is the ruling ethical motif.

We must see the error of concluding that *all* ethical declarations are intended for *all* individuals in *all* circumstances and without regard for the special conditions that prompted those declarations in the first place. What Scripture means in one place must be gauged by what Scripture says elsewhere. Otherwise we can be charged with indiscriminate handling of God's Word. This study seeks diligently to avoid that trap.

A familiar mind-set among evangelicals is the preference for tightly defined dogmas. The more one can pin down a specific text "to say it all," the better one likes it. We are not comfortable with ambiguities, with gray areas. We prefer to take what God says on a single occasion and universalize it to cover all cases somewhat similar, regardless of differences. We like to reinforce our presuppositions. And if for years we have proclaimed certain dogmas as absolute truth, can we dare now admit that we have changed our thinking? Tough going for evangelicals!

The author's intent is not to dogmatize, to coerce others to conform their thinking to his, but rather to demonstrate as skillfully as possible that the Bible is not a code book with rules for every situation. Paul wrote in 2 Corinthians 3:5–6: ". . . our competence is from God, who has made us competent to be ministers of a new covenant, not in a written code but in the Spirit; for the written code kills, but the Spirit gives life." We need to have the Spirit infuse new life into our thinking upon this most wrenching of subjects! Legalism has been tried and found wanting; prohibition is obviously not the answer. So let us move boldly, yet not presumptuously, into the freedom of God's grace! May the Lord make us truly competent to apply His Word in redemptive realism to complex situations in our time. Can we not afford to forsake party lines that cripple evangelicalism enough as it is? Shall we not relinquish the inflexibility that is safe but wrong? Let us dare to be biblical, yet biblical in the larger framework of Scripture's incomparable teaching. Yes, may we do our exegesis well, but then be wise and put each passage under the light of the best theological ethics we know. Let us be fully contextual, not content to view passages in isolation. We need to have eyes to see the ethical progression in Scripture, no longer constrained by the erroneous presupposition that every New Testament ethical statement can be lifted out of context and universalized to fit *all* persons in *all* circumstances at *all* times and places. Let us unashamedly embrace the grace of God's loving, provisional will for less-than-perfect saints!

If we require further illustration of these principles, the most obvious is the Old Testament Mosaic law from which New Testament believers are now set free. No longer, for example, are we commanded to stone to death those who are guilty of adultery. In full accord with God's grace in Christ, we seek to lead them to a saving knowledge of the Redeemer. The glorious good news is this: "And such were some of you. But you were washed, you were sanctified, you were justified in the name of the Lord Jesus Christ and in the Spirit of our God" (1 Cor. 6:11). *It is, you see, grace, not law; redemption, not condemnation; renewal, not prohibition!*

From Mosaic Law to Kingdom Ethics

Much of the confusion as to how we are to interpret Jesus' sayings is due to the fact that He often spoke as One standing within the confines of Mosaic law. Time and again He related what He said to the ethical context of the Old Testament, not going outside it. This accounts for the fact that so much of what we read in the Gospel records does not reappear in the same form in the Epistles written to instruct the life of the church. The Old Covenant with all its provisions, including the law, waited for fulfillment in Jesus' death and resurrection. Nor could the new principles of life by grace be understood, much less implemented, until the risen Christ had ascended to the Father and sent the Holy Spirit to be the indwelling illumination and power for this new life. Since Pentecost there is a new ethical administration, and there is also a new power to fulfill the kingdom ethic in daily living. Still there is the overarching problem of an imperfect fulfillment in the church, of human failure. It is this that makes divorce and remarriage a continuing fact in the Christian community. It is to focus on this problem that this book has been written.

In light of the principles of grace expounded in the Epistles especially, are we being consistent to proclaim on one hand the free and full pardon of all sin, the wiping clean of the slate, while at the same time insisting that one failure alone—marital failure—be penalized and stigmatized? Is it not cruelly incongruous with our doctrine of forgiveness to insist that divorce is unpardonable and normal life unrestorable—to the extent that divorced persons can never again contract a loving marriage, never enjoy another life partner, never live happily in the intimate society called family, never again hold office or serve significantly in the church of our gracious Redeemer? Have we the right to assign a lesser status to divorced Christians, singling them out as less acceptable than other Christians who acknowledge equally serious failure (or even more so)? These questions must deeply trouble every mature and sensitive Christian—especially those called to the pastoral or counseling ministry.

On what grounds shall our final determination of the matter be made? On statements made in restricted and unusual contexts? On Jesus' focused reply to the Pharisees who sought to trap Him in the interpretation of Mosaic law? On Paul's particular response to particular questions, asked by a particular church in Corinth in a particularly abnormal time? Or shall we take the larger view, placing all these elements of the subject together with what we know of the New Testament's ruling ethic of grace, and then approach individual cases with a sanctified judgment born of this process? Are we able to live out the freedom of new beginnings in the grace of Christ without presuming upon God's gift? Are we able to order our lives in responsible freedom under the leadership of Jesus Christ and within the ethical guidelines of the New Testament? This is no easy road, but it appears to this author as the only road.

Inasmuch as one of the statements of Jesus with reference to divorce and remarriage comes in what we know as the Sermon on the Mount, it is necessary to come to some understanding as to how we place the radicalized, absolute form of ethics found there together with the ethic of grace that appears uniquely in the church Epistles. This is a major undertaking, but it is crucial to our developing position. In the Sermon, we have the perfect righteousness of God set forth as superior to the law of Moses. This is the righteousness that will prevail in absolute fashion when the kingdom of God is established upon earth under the reign of the returning King. It may be characterized as "works-righteousness" and is accompanied, not by promises of grace, but by severe judgments for noncompliance. It is not accompanied by any teaching concerning redemptive grace and forgiveness. Then what are we to make of this absolute ethic for ourselves? Is it a new law, handed down at the very time Jesus is preparing to sacrifice Himself in order to deliver us from the law of Moses? If it is the law of absolute righteousness that will prevail in the coming kingdom, how then do we adapt it (as surely we must) to the conditions that prevail throughout the church age? Can we say that for us, struggling in a fallen world, it is presently not so much "law" as "moral ideal"—God's direction to us, although possible of limited fulfillment only? Upon this question hinges the whole question of how God deals with incomplete fulfillment and outright failure. Specifically, how does God deal with marital failure? These are not easy questions except for those who choose easy answers. So critical an issue is our interpretation of the Sermon on the Mount that chapter nine is devoted to it.

Reality of an Imperfect Church

You can readily see what motivates the author to write this treatise. For Christians, the utter joy of being pardoned is to be set free forever from two things—*penalty and guilt*! But, sadly, even if God gives divorced Christians who have penitently sought His best no further reason for guilt, most likely the evangelical community will! If God exacts no penalty, the church in many instances does! Even when willful sin does not appear to be present in a given divorce situation, the church too eagerly treats it as though somehow or other this *must* be so. How curious indeed that we ask for marriage success on the part of all couples, despite the fact that with respect to no other ethical absolute can the church produce an unblemished record of success. Thus the church's problem becomes that of unrealistic expectations. Of course, the church, with scriptural warrant, proclaims the sufficiency of Christ and the power of the Holy Spirit for all human problems. However, we tend to translate this into expectations of success in every instance. No Christian would deny that the power of Christ is available to all believers. It is equally true that His power is sufficient to heal all who are afflicted physically or emotionally, to secure jobs for all who have such need. But does this always follow? Of course not. We face the limitations of believers to appropriate fully the resources they have in God. What about the matter of Christian maturity, or the availability and adequacy of Christian counsel, or the extremity of conditions assaulting marital relationships? Beyond even these considerations lies the deep mystery of why God in His sovereignty does not answer the faith of *all* who seek healing, *all* who need jobs, *all* whose children are outside the faith, *all* who cannot make marriage what God intends.

Any pastor is aware of marriages that are nothing short of "impossible." For understandable reasons, some of these marriages have been impossible from the day they began. Haste and immaturity, along with romantic expectations, account for many mismatches. Yet there are pastors who choose to believe that people must remain in impossible marriages, regardless of damage done to themselves and to their children. As though God delights in a status quo of failure and torture—as though He desires a formal marriage contract to prevail over the very welfare of those who are sinking under a totally destructive relationship. There are teachers today, some quite prominent, who rationalize the continuance of such suffering—even suffering that probably can never change—as being a positive Christian experience. Simply suffer your impossible marriage "for Jesus' sake," they say. You need not end the torture, destruction, and despair—wear a halo instead!

Marriage Made for Man— Or Man for Marriage?

Is God bound to laws of His own making, or may His actions sometimes transcend those laws, as in instances where those laws would render compassionate, redeeming grace inoperable? We are not considering some form of leniency or toleration or compromise. By "grace" we mean God's provisional will, His redemptive response to man's failure. Marriage was made for man, not man for marriage. Thus it is a mistake to think that the welfare of individuals must always be subordinated to the marriage institution, as though its legal claims always supersede claims to personal well-being. Not at all. God considers our welfare. *Marriage serves man, not man marriage.* This principle is fundamental to our understanding of the proper place of divorce and remarriage.

In coming to grips with God's truth, we recognize and respect the fact that there are divergent views abroad. But it does no one any good to say that there are half a dozen prominent views—so take your choice and hope you are right. This book takes a definite position; it is grace-oriented throughout. And it is written with the intelligent lay person in mind. It will accordingly not be our method always to cite biblical authorities or other sources. The reader has probably suffered enough without having to suffer the citation of authorities! The value of the book must rest ultimately with how well it speaks to the reader's own study of God's Word and whether it makes sense theologically.

From participation in scores of pastors' conferences and marriage workshops across the land, the author is persuaded that the dark shroud we hang on all divorce is largely of our own making. We are right in abhoring divorce as such, especially the more notorious causes for it. We hate the consequences that follow in the wake of many divorces, though not all. But we might well take greater concern with why the church has responded so late and so poorly to the needs of the divorced. Where is the redemptive arm of the church? We have been strangely insensitive to the loneliness of a life suddenly severed from the family community. We are almost embarrassed to think about the sexual needs abruptly rendered unfulfillable. We look upon the divorced with suspicion, as though they must surely be predatory creatures with eyes only for the wife or husband of another. They become the untouchables. Somehow the liberating friendship of an accepting fellowship of God's people has not reached out in the same way that Jesus reached out to the woman taken in adultery (John 8:1–11). Although He cited the law's condemnation to her, He acted in grace not judgment. He granted the accusation of her accusers but offered her forgiveness. He mentioned no penalties, imposed no prohibitions or sanctions. *She was free—free because forgiven!* This forgiveness meant freedom to begin again; the past had lost its dark importance altogether! Jesus' only word to her as He sent her on her way was, "Go, and sin no more." Does He appoint us to anything less, pastor friend? Is this not a clue?

Looking Ahead

There is a biblical right of divorce and remarriage, but it is not an option in accord with God's design and purpose. *Strictly speaking, it is not a right at all.* No such right can be found in the orders of creation. Under Mosaic law, it was a right that God granted as a concession of grace, an expression of His provisional will for a fallen people. In Jesus' teaching, He indicated that in God's original design for marriage there could be no divorce; marriage was to be permanent and exclusive between two people, hence indissoluble. Yet He conceded that in man's fallenness there is an intrinsically justifiable exception—when adultery has been committed against one's spouse. Remarriage is tantamount to "ethical adultery"—a term we shall explain in due course—for remarriage violates God's creative intent that there be but one sexual partner so long as the two are alive. This was Jesus' reply to those who asked if Mosaic law permitted divorce for any cause. The answer, like the question, was limited to this particular context. In the church age of grace, the interim before the kingdom is established in its fullness, this judgment is most likely not to be applied as prohibitive law, but as the guiding ideal for fulfilling the highest will of God. Inasmuch as some will fail to meet the divine standard, God's will is provisional. In grace, God accommodates to the weakness, sin, and failure of His children. Although never God's pure intention, divorce and remarriage nonetheless come within His provisional will for a church where spiritual and moral incapability still takes its toll. God has always acted toward His people in grace, but never more fully than in this church age of grace. Divine governance through grace has its special characteristics during this interim period.

The sole passage on divorce and remarriage in the Epistles is Paul's word to the Corinthian church in answer to some specific questions relating to their situation at the time—a time of "impending distress." Paul's answer may very well not extend beyond their particular circumstances. In all likelihood, it is not intended to be universalized as God's final word to the church universal. This is a major question to be taken up at length later on.[1]

It is a curious fact that so little is taught on divorce and remarriage in the Epistles, inasmuch as the problem of our day was perfectly known to the Author of Scripture. What do we conclude from that fact? Possibly that enough direction has been given to enable our seeking the mind of the Spirit in order to make wise pastoral decisions—or personal ones, as the case may be. This, too, will require more attention later on.

---

1. We do not regard Romans 7:1–4 as relevant to the subject. Reasons for this are taken up in Appendix A.

Hinge of History

A considerable part of the argument of this book revolves around the manner in which God administers His will during the church age, when the kingdom ethic is in effect but when His people are not always capable of fulfilling it as it shall be in the established kingdom. It may be helpful at the very beginning to say a word about this, to see it in historical perspective. We must familiarize ourselves with the *transition* from Israel under Mosaic law to the church under redeeming grace. This transition took place over a prolonged period, dated from early in Jesus' ministry and running throughout the period covered by the Book of Acts—the beginnings of the church. This period ended with the destruction of Jerusalem and the turning of the apostles to the Gentiles.

The words of Jesus relating to divorce and remarriage come in the period when His message was still directed to Israel only, and when the message of ethical perfection looked to the future kingdom. In neither set of Gospel references to divorce did Jesus have the church interim period in mind, except indirectly. God's ethical governance during the church interim was disclosed later, as expounded in the Epistles. So we have both historical and developmental reasons for understanding why Jesus did not address the question of God's ethical administration for our time in the divorce passages in the Gospels. Here we have an illustration of how not everything is necessarily taught on a single occasion, or when listeners are unprepared for more than they are given. We must always stop and make certain who is and who is not being addressed, and for what purposes. Would we be addressed in exactly the same manner? Of this we must make absolutely sure.

The very idea of such a historical and ethical transition may be unfamiliar to some readers. It is common for people to ask, "But isn't the church the kingdom on earth now?" The answer is *yes* and *no. The church is not the kingdom; the two are not identical.* Neither is the church establishing the kingdom as an earthly entity. However, the church is directly related to the kingdom and represents the kingdom during this age. Christian believers, participants in the church, are indeed citizens of the kingdom, which is yet to come. The ethics of the kingdom are set before the church as God's perfect way of righteousness and hence are the ethic for our time. But we are not under the personal reign of a ruling messianic King. Neither do we occupy our resurrection bodies. Satan is not yet bound but remains "the god of this world." Our carnal nature still leads us into defeats. And so we must come to terms with the present reality, namely, that along with kingdom ethics—especially its radicalized form in the Sermon on the Mount—is our inability to perfectly fulfill the ethical demands. This ethic is accompanied by judgments, yet we know that in the age of grace we are not subject to such judgments. The ethic of grace as presently administered alters that aspect altogether.

One hint of the great transition from law to grace is given in John 1:17—"For the law was given through Moses; grace and truth came through Jesus Christ." The transition came before Pentecost, although it was on that great day that the Holy Spirit came to baptize believers into the body of Christ and to indwell them with His powerful presence, enabling believers to live as God commands them to live. The problem is not that we lack adequate resources to so live, but that we fail to appropriate them at times or to appropriate them fully. At other times we succumb to the forces that work against us.

It would be easy to assume that readers are familiar with what we mean by God's grace. A working definition should prove helpful: *Grace is God's freely given, unmerited favor toward the sinful and failing, the expression of forgiving, redeeming, restoring love toward the unworthy.* Let us examine this briefly so that the basic ideas are clear as we move along.

Grace arises from God's unconditional love, a love with no strings attached, no preconditions for its action. Grace is God's love taking the initiative to meet our need, whatever that need may be. God does not love us for anything He can gain from His loving; it is not based on some kind of exchange system. In no way does He love us because we are deserving or have earned it. He loves us and reaches out to us in grace simply because the nature of love is to reach out caringly. He loves the unlovely, the sinner, the one who cannot possibly merit that love. So it is a divine love, which cannot be enhanced by our goodness or diminished by our badness. To love the unlovely is God's great delight! To lavish undeserved favor is His joy!

God has set His heart upon us; He made us in His image, and He wills to restore us to that image. His way is suffering, redemptive love, willingness to pay whatever price is necessary to reconcile us to Himself and to lavish His best upon us. Such love is merciful and forgiving. It is creative—creative of a returning love, creative of a grateful heart. Such love creates in us new incentives to live to God's glory, to resist evil. And not only does God's love save us by this grace-principle; it leads us along, providing for our every need and ever renewing us when we fall. This is the love, the grace, the forgiving and renewing nature of God's dealing with His growing but still imperfect children. His love remains provisional, able to accommodate itself to whatever need arises. Divine love is neither inflexible nor incapable of adapting itself to failure, whether that failure be partial or complete. Love does not give up; it patiently moves to secure new life and new capability in all in whom that love has made itself known. Love does not withdraw in the face of failure or sin, and this is the love that met us at first in the very reality of our lost and sinful condition. Divine love gives itself to facilitate whatever promotes the highest welfare of those within its care. So it is the love of God in Christ that is the ever-present condition in the equation. It is this love we experience as God's forgiving, renewing grace. It is this love, this grace, that mediates between God's purpose and the human condition that reflects a failure to fulfill God's purpose. Whatever state we are in, and however we got there, love keeps a door open to renewal. To understand God's dealing with unpreventable divorce is to first understand the nature of His love and grace.

2

Covenant of Unity and Fidelity

To ask, "What is the meaning of divorce?" before we have answered the prior question, "What is the meaning of Christian marriage?" is to preclude the possibility of really understanding divorce. The theology of marriage precedes the ethics of divorce simply because divorce repudiates and cancels something we call marriage. Just what is it that is being dissolved, and what dissolves it? What is divorce besides something we can define legally? This chapter is basic to our entire study, inasmuch as it addresses these questions.

In seminars with young couples over the years and in my marriage course at Westmont College, I have asked repeatedly, "What is the nature and meaning of Christian marriage?" In pastors' conferences, the question has been posed in a slightly different manner: "What do you teach young couples about the multifaceted meaning of Christian marriage?" The range and diversity of the answers never cease to amaze me. Most responses lack depth of scriptural understanding; there is little if any theological underpinning. That Americans have to a large extent trivialized marriage—a process aided by the media—is a sad fact of modern life. There is truth in the quip, "We wouldn't get divorced for such trivial reasons if we didn't get married for such trivial reasons." It recalls the recent cartoon depicting a newlywed couple just arrived at their honeymoon hotel. The bride, still in her wedding dress, says, "Harold, I want a divorce. I found someone else in the reception line." Or how about the *avant-garde* counselor who got his kicks from saying, "Be sure to plan your wedding for morning; if it doesn't work out, you won't have blown the whole day!" And so, on every hand, it seems marriage is subject to trivialization.

Sad to say, Christians are not immune to this trivialization. Of the young we expect a certain immaturity, and unfortunately it is mainly the young who first enter marriage. Yet, older couples are often hard put to come up with adequate answers as to what Christian marriage means. Evidently our generation is not being taught God's holy purposes for marriage, and widespread failure is perfectly understandable.

Although Scripture is neither as complete nor direct on this subject as we could wish, with diligence we can trace the basic ideas. What we learn has far-reaching importance. Scripture provides, *first,* a concept of personal, spiritual meaning, and *second,* a husband-wife role structure. Both the nature of the relationship and its proper functioning are His appointment. Thus the biblical design contains two equally important parts. First, marriage is a covenant of unity and fidelity. Second, it is founded upon a mandate for marital roles. As we know very well, grasping God's purpose understandingly can not in itself guarantee marital success. But if Christian marriage is to be as successful as God planned it to be, this is the sure foundation upon which it must be built. Do it God's way or the warranty is void.

Is Marriage a Sacrament?

Roman Catholics say *yes;* Protestants *no.* Before we can consider the significance of this question, crucial as we shall see it to be, we must first understand what a sacrament is and what it is not, according to Scripture and Reformed theology.

The word *sacrament* is not found in Scripture. It is a theological term standing for an external act that represents an inward spiritual reality, and it is always associated with the covenant of grace. A workable definition might read as follows: *A sacrament is a holy ordinance instituted by God for His covenant community, the church, in which by visible signs God's grace in salvation is represented and sealed to the recipient.* It is sign and seal of a spiritual reality. Its enactment certifies or ratifies God's covenant gift of salvation and man's response. By means of a sacrament, the truth addressed to man's ear by the Word of God is symbolically expressed to man's eye. Sacraments confirm God's Word and act, serving thus as a means of grace and as aids to human sensibility. The sacrament enacts God's pledge and man's response. God pledges Himself to us by both Word and Sign. The sacrament thus certifies to both parties, God and man, that they are under covenant obligations to one another and that these are binding obligations. The sacrament becomes a visible ratification of God's pledge to man and man's response of faith. The sacraments attest to a divine covenant that cannot be abrogated.

In New Testament teaching, two sacraments—and only two—are shown to have been instituted by our Lord. They are of two distinct types—initiatory and commemorative. "Initiatory" means it is enacted *once* in relation to each individual believer. Baptism is an initiatory sacrament, representing once and for all the relationship of the believer to Christ, the believer's death to sin and resurrection to newness of life in Christ. It ratifies, as it were, the believer's inclusion within the covenant of salvation and incorporation into Christ as a member of His body. At the same time, from the believer's standpoint, it certifies faith in Jesus' saving death. So baptism is "initiatory"—sign and seal of a one-time transaction, the faith-reception of salvation.

The other sacrament, the Lord's Supper, is "commemorative," celebrated frequently to commemorate the Lord's death on our behalf and signifying the believer's union with Christ. When the sacrament is accompanied by faith, the believer partakes of Christ, the Living Bread, and Christ communicates Himself in special grace. The Lord's Supper is a remembrance made visible. Both sacraments concern the redemptive work of Christ as it is applied to the believer in the covenant of salvation.

Marriage, sacred as it is and as surely instituted by God, is nevertheless *not* a sacrament, nor is it intended to be. Contrary to Roman Catholic teaching, marriage was not instituted as a sacrament by our Lord. Protestants speak of marriage as a "sacred institution," and this it most certainly is. This distinction is crucial to our understanding, for the very possibility of divorce and remarriage hinges upon this doctrinal difference. Catholic influence upon Protestant thinking at this point must be rejected. Marriage is a covenant, not a sacrament.

If we were to say that marriage is indeed a sacrament, then the very act of marriage would signify an irrevocable enactment between God and the married couple. Marriage, in God's eyes, would then be indissoluble. It would remain indissoluble whatever might occur between the couple, whether or not they were faithful to their vows, whether or not they sought to establish and maintain a biblically directed marriage. So, if marriage is a divine enactment established forever at the wedding (wedding plus sexual consummation), then divorce is impermissible under any circumstance. What this view really says is that marriage is a reality apart from any continuing behavior of husband and wife, apart from either their actions or their attitudes. Whether their marriage is marked by fidelity or infidelity, love or non-love, unity or total disunity, response to biblically mandated roles or not, that marriage is an irrevocably established reality that cannot change. Thus the marital bond is totally unrelated to human action; it does not take personal acts of either husband or wife into consideration in its claim to permanence. As a sacramental reality, it would remain that forever, unalterable in its essence.

Now, quite oppositely, if marriage is *not* a sacrament, not a divine enactment, but a sacred covenant that looks to God's confirmation and blessing, then it is a reality dependent indeed upon the spouses' continuing affirmation. Its reality depends not only upon what was initiated at the beginning but equally upon what the couple sustains from there on. Christian marriage rests upon more than an initial covenant; it rests upon the fidelity of each spouse to the other—fidelity to all that is incorporated into their covenant unity. This is an absolute requisite if we are to be able to say of any given marriage, "What God has joined together. . . ." For, you see, it is possible—frighteningly possible—for men and women married to each other to violate or even repudiate altogether their marriage-covenant obligations. Especially is this compounded if Christians do not even recognize their marriage as having covenant obligations that are biblically mandated. Clearly, covenant keeping is vulnerable to all the intricate possibilities of human sin and failure.

It must be asked, "How did this misunderstanding of marriage as 'sacrament' arise? Was it present from the beginning?"

In the early church, marriages were not performed in churches, nor were ministers marriage officiants. Is that surprising? In those times, Christians were not even required to seek the blessing of the church to give validity to their marriage. Only later did it become a customary practice to have a Christian ceremony in which the church confirmed the marriage and sealed it with a benediction. Marriage was not a sacrament.

Marriage doctrine took a major turn with Saint Augustine, who contended that marriage *was* a sacrament. It was the massive influence of Augustine that determined the doctrine of the Western church. He based his concept of marriage as a sacrament upon his interpretation of Ephesians 5:21–33. Marriage is a human enactment of the same essence as Christ's marriage to His bride, the church. Augustine argued, "Did not our Lord indissolubly bond Himself to His church in saving grace?" From this truth Augustine drew a false inference: *As Christ is indissolubly bonded to His church, what is true of His relationship to His bride must also be true of all married couples; they, too, are indissolubly bonded.*

Later on, the church mistranslated the word *mysterion* (mystery) to mean "sacrament," strengthening the premise that marriage is sacramental. The covenant bond between Christ and His church became more than mere analogy, more than sacred model; the marriage bond came to represent the indissoluble bond between Christ and His church. Consequently, the marriage bond cannot be broken any more than the bond between Christ and His church can be broken. From this premise came the doctrine of indissolubility.

Now, what might have been truly perceived as covenant obligations between married partners—a union dissoluble whenever those covenant obligations were not met—was perceived instead as a sacramental bond, a divine enactment. This assumption altered the whole understanding of marriage and its essence. Dissolubility was impossible; in practice, divorce was impermissible. In the Roman Catholic Church to this day, this thinking prevails as official doctrine. Curiously, from earliest times, only the Western branch of the church held that marriage is indissoluble; the Eastern branch did not. Early on, the Eastern church recognized the validity of remarriage after divorce.

Protestants, rejecting the notion of marriage as sacrament, see Ephesians 5:21–33 as an analogy, a sacred sign but no more than that. The marriage union is truly to represent the union between Christ and His church and to model this union in its permanence and fidelity to covenant obligations.

Up to this point there is little difference between Catholic and Protestant positions. But here the ways part; marriage is not a divine enactment with binding obligations to God. It is a sacred institution that invites God's blessing upon it. It has a right to expect God's blessing as, and only as, each spouse seeks to fulfill the biblical mandate for a Christian marriage. For marriages taking place in the church, with a minister as officiant, couples manifest their intent that their union be blessed by God. It is a sacred act.

There is one further distinction relating to sacraments. The two sacraments that Jesus instituted have to do with an eternal relationship between Himself and His believing community. But marriage does not stand for an eternally unchanged relationship, for Jesus Himself said that there is no marriage in heaven. Salvation is an eternal relationship based on a covenant between God and man, but marriage is an earth-time relationship based on a covenant between the married partners.

Marriage, we believe correctly, is seen by Protestants as a covenant, subject to the conditions governing covenants between human beings—for this is what marriage covenants are. Such covenants can be violated, even repudiated altogether. For this reason, divorce is both possible and permissible under certain conditions. True, for some Protestants divorce is not permissible, but their grounds are other than the inviolable character of a sacrament. We shall consider this further on.

Scriptural Warrant for Marriage as Covenant

In both Old and New Testaments, marriage is described in covenant terms. In the Old Testament, the covenant analogy is that between God and His people Israel. One of the more explicit references is Malachi 2:14: "The LORD was witness to the covenant between you and the wife of your youth. . . ." *It is important to our understanding that it is a covenant between marriage partners, not between them and God; God is witness to the covenant between partners.* Marriage vows are not made to God, but to each other in His presence—calling Him to be witness to their pledge of troth to each other.

In the New Testament, marriage follows the analogy of Christ and His church. In both Testaments, the covenant of grace that God made with His people is commonly expressed in terms of His marriage with His people. So, in reciprocal fashion, on one hand marriage conveys the meaning of covenant, and on the other the covenant conveys the meaning of marriage. The reverse side of this is the image of infidelity used to describe the sin of covenant breaking (see Jer. 2:20ff.).

Covenant obligations within married life are patterned

after the relationship between Christ and His church. Further on we shall see that this pattern takes on a specific role structure as well. The essential nature of the covenant relationship is that of unity and fidelity. The heart of the covenant is commitment to certain obligations, and that commitment implies lifelong fidelity, or marital permanence. But there are other obligations of equal importance.

We must not view this covenant abstractly, for the divine model shows the nature of the covenant to be that of *loving mutuality* and *reciprocal servanthood*—each spouse lovingly serving the other. So intimate is this bond of unity that Paul turns to the language of Genesis, to the order of creation, and speaks of a married couple as being "one flesh." Later on in our study we shall find that this term speaks of the union of persons in their total personhood, not just the physical unity achieved in intercourse.[1] The finest summary statement I know relative to this point is that of Geoffrey Bromiley: "As God made man in His own image, so He made earthly marriage in the image of His own eternal marriage with His people." What a sacred imaging our marriages are intended to be! What intimacy and faithfulness this implies! What a totality this union is to represent!

Some writers, such as Jay Adams, refer to the covenant as "the covenant of companionship," but this is inadequate. It picks up on but one dimension of the covenant bond; it is far more than that. "Companionship" could mean no more than friendship, a more casual relationship, one not necessarily permanent or exclusive. It does not carry the meaning of either fidelity or unity. Nor does the word *companionship* embrace the relationship in its totality, as comprehended by the "one flesh" terminology. The obligations of unity and fidelity are far greater than those of even the most meaningful companionship. This is the fundamental deficiency of living together outside of marriage.

As God's covenant with His people is a pledge of fidelity, so couples employ vows that give public expression to their

---

1. For a full exposition of the "one flesh" concept, see the author's book *Christian, Celebrate Your Sexuality* (Old Tappan, NJ: Fleming H. Revell, 1974).

pledge of fidelity to one another. Vows express commitment, or intent at least. They pledge one's loyalty to covenant obligations. Lewis Smedes puts it succinctly: "The single ingredient that stamps a sexual partnership as a marriage is fidelity." He then interprets fidelity as lifelong commitment, adding "A vow is an act of trust in the face of an unpredictable future." While, as he notes, no one knows for sure how a marriage is going to work out, spouses *can* know for sure what are the intentions upon which they have founded their marriage. It is their responsibility to make this determination at the very start. They begin with intention and hope, setting a course and undertaking responsibilities that will give marriage its form and direction. But fidelity to vows, as Smedes notes, can only be as lasting as fidelity to each other as persons. Add to this their concern to represent the covenant of which Christ is both Model and invited Partner. The continuing question should then be, "Is our marriage a representation of the love, unity, and fidelity that characterize the relationship between Christ and His bride, the church?" Anything less falls short of being Christian marriage on New Testament terms. This is the bedrock biblical ideal.

All of this has far-reaching implications, not the least of which is the willingness of each spouse to relinquish his or her independent self-life in continuing acts of self-surrender for their mutual welfare. Each spouse thereby is free to live as other-directed, to seek wholeness in the marital bond. In practical terms, it is a covenant of intercommunication at all levels of personal existence. This, too, is what it means to be "one flesh."

Implicit in the word *cleave* in Genesis 2:24 is the notion of permanence, exclusivity, and fidelity. The word meaning of "cleave" is established in such passages as Deuteronomy 10:20: "You shall fear the LORD your God; you shall serve him and cleave to him. . . ." Or Psalm 119:31: "I cleave to thy testimonies, O LORD. . . ." In a day that exalts self-sufficiency, self-directedness, and self-fulfillment, Christian marriage calls us to full interdependence with our spouses. Mutual servanthood also has its opposite side: mutual need. It is no advantage in marriage for spouses to pretend they do not really need each other. Indeed, this point of view is diametrically opposed to the scriptural idea of mutual servanthood. Spouses are to bear each other's burdens and meet each other's needs in so far as this is possible. Should a couple succeed in pretending they do not need each other, they will find one day that they are subconsciously seeking fulfillment of unrecognized needs by turning elsewhere. Then the very covenant of unity and fidelity becomes obscured, and trouble lies close at hand.

What should we say about the vows we make to each other? Human beings are incapable of pledging absolutes. This includes absolute vows in marriage. It is impossible to say, "I'll love you forever." That is something we cannot say. What we can say and mean with all our hearts is: "I want to love you forever. I am trusting God to enable me to be able to love you forever. With His help this is my hope and expectation." That is all we can say, but we can say that. Similarly, we cannot say, "Our marriage will last forever." What we can say is: "I now commit myself to our marriage, and with God's help I expect to make it last forever." As sincere as we may be—and this is not the question—our frail humanity prevents us from making absolute pledges. And does not God know this far better than we ourselves?

When a young couple starts out in their first experiences of marriage, their vows may be as sincerely made as ever could be expected. They have no intention whatever of making them conditional or tentative. All the reinforcement of a powerful early love carries them forward with confidence. Little can they know what lies ahead, yet courageously they express their trust in an unforeseeable future. So far as they know, their pledge rests upon a commitment grounded in love. They are certain that their marriage will endure because they are persuaded that their love will endure. They cannot foresee the possibilities outside or inside themselves that have the power to alter that love or place barriers between them. Therefore, absolute promises are given and received with a simple and sometimes naive assurance. It is not to their discredit that they have no previous experience of married life preparing them to foresee the dangers ahead. Their intuition tells them it would be a betrayal of love to think even for a moment that the day might come when their love would die, and along with it the commitment grounded in that love.

David Atkinson in Great Britain takes a cue from Lewis Smedes, and it is a sound one. He places emphasis upon covenant faithfulness as a positive action, not a negative one: "The model of creative, covenant faithfulness seen in the steadfast love and faithfulness of God, indicates that faithfulness in marriage can and should be something positive, creative and dynamic—much more than the avoidance of adultery." If, as Smedes says, "Positive fidelity is first of all a dedication to the freedom, maturity and growth of the other person," then may we not say as well that unfaithfulness is the refusal to be a facilitator of the freedom, the maturity, and the growth of the other? Covenant fidelity, patterned after the covenant between Christ and the church, is indeed positive and creative, aiming for the highest welfare of one's spouse and jealous to maintain covenant integrity at whatever personal cost.

Carried to its logical conclusion, covenant faithfulness is fully realized only within an exclusive, lifelong relationship. Permanence, as Atkinson cogently insists, is not merely an ideal; it is a premise. If marriage is conceived as a true and dynamic representation of covenant unity and fidelity, patterned after that of Christ and the church, then there can be no question but that permanence is the premise. From the human perspective it may be the ideal; from God's perspective it is the premise.

When Is the Covenant Breached?

Any unfaithfulness to covenant obligations, that is, any breaking faith in a significant sense, places the covenant in jeopardy. It is a short step to outright violation, even repudiation of the covenant altogether. A covenant of unity and fidelity may be breached overtly or covertly—in words or

actions, but also in thought or attitude. This covenant
breach may be external or internal, observable to others or
not. Adultery, upon which we tend to place such singular
emphasis, represents an external breach. Curiously, we talk
as though adultery were the only possible breach of covenant fidelity! This is natural enough, inasmuch as it follows from the single exception Jesus acknowledged in His
debate with the Pharisees over the legality of Mosaic provisions for divorce. But this can be misleading. Covenant
unity and fidelity can be breached in many destructive
ways, many of them neither as obvious nor flagrant as adultery. Many are internal, with little or no visibility. *Whenever
a spouse is aware of being no longer committed to covenant
goals or obligations, to marital unity as total partnership, or
to a loving mutuality, then the covenant is beginning to come
apart.* For an initial period at least, the process is reversible.
It may be known only to the one who is secretly pulling
away. But if left to continue, the process becomes irreversible in time—except for God's intervention. For some couples
this intervening grace of God is gloriously experienced, and
the marriage is saved; the covenant is not irreparably
breached. How fervently we could wish that this were experienced by every couple!

A recently divorced couple explained, "We firmly believe
that marriage is 'till death do us part.' Our marriage died,
so we parted." This, of course, pretty well misconstrues the
meaning of the traditional phrase. It demonstrates, however, how easily a couple can mouth familiar words while
missing their meaning. *Yet, seriously, there is a sense in
which marriages can die.* Covenant unity can be broken because one or both spouses walk away from its obligations or
turn off mentally or emotionally in what becomes tantamount to a repudiation of the covenant. All too often an internal repudiation precedes the more visible external
conflict. Deep-seated alienation can arise gradually, for instance, out of an emotionally barren relationship. Resentment can turn into bitter hate over time. The covenant
ceases to exist.

It comes down to the choices we make, or continue to make.
We choose to remain faithful to the covenant—or not to. We
all make a choice at the very beginning and continue to
make choices all along the way. Faithless actions and attitudes often precede by some length of time that moment
when it all spills over into a new attraction, say, or an extra-
marital affair. Sexual infidelity then is symptom, not cause.
Divorce then merely gives decent burial to the marriage
that died—or was murdered!

Divorce Is Absolute

When we perceive the meaning of marriage in terms of a
covenant of unity and fidelity—mutuality based on love and
reciprocal servanthood—it is apparent immediately that divorce is the total dismantling of the covenant. No longer has
the covenant any real existence. It is as though it had never
existed at all. Everything that previously was attributable
to the covenant relationship has ceased to be. This should
make us forever clear about the absoluteness of divorce.
Nothing of covenant obligations, rights, or privileges continues. It is patently false to say that a couple, although divorced, is "still married in the sight of God." What possibly
exists in the eyes of God that has not been dissolved by the
absolute negation of the covenant?

When Christ admonishes us not to put asunder what God
has joined together, the implication is, of course, that man
can do just that! Christ does not ask us to "not do" what, in
fact, cannot be done! And the very term indicates a total and
complete break. This, incidentally, is the only way in which
Deuteronomy 24:1–4 can be understood. There, when the
wife leaves her first husband, she becomes "the wife of another" who is called "her husband." In fact, the point of the
passage is that the first husband "may not take her again to
be his wife." To say, then, that a couple is still married in
God's sight although divorced makes nonsense out of this
passage. This applies throughout Scripture.

Are Marriages of Christians "Christian" Marriages?

The answer is "Sometimes, but not always." This may seem a radical charge to make, but we do not hesitate to make it. Can we possibly say that a marriage is truly Christian although made with no understanding of, or commitment to, the covenant of unity and fidelity that is representative of that which Christ made with His church? I doubt it! However, I fear the responsibility for this deficiency lies with the church, for it seems that all too often the church in its teaching and practice treats marriage as little more than the vows two people make to each other out of a love experience, a romantic relationship that is blessed by the church and legitimized by registration with the state. After all, they are nice young people and come from solid church-going families. They are sincere and want the church's blessing. They expect their love to see them through, and they do not believe in divorce. Is this not enough to mark it as a Christian marriage? Hardly!

Yet I cannot come down hard on my fellow pastors. For many years my own teaching and practice left much to be desired on that score. But let us begin, if begin afresh we must, to teach that marriage is a covenant embracing the total personhood of two people, a covenant representative of Christ and His church, a covenant of caring love and fidelity, the ultimate proof of which is a lifelong commitment to carry out the covenant obligations as set forth in Scripture. Then perhaps when a young couple says, "Pastor, we want you to tie the knot," we will not feel like answering, "What kind of knot do you have in mind—a square knot or a slip knot?"

Biblical Mandate for Marital Roles

At the beginning of this chapter we suggested that the biblical view of marriage has two distinct and equally important parts. We come now to the second part—husband-and-wife role structure and role differentiation. Like the first part, this teaching is found in Ephesians 5:21–33. It is a mandate that Christian husbands and wives must view with utmost seriousness, especially since it runs counter to our natural inclinations.

In every marriage there is role structure, a pattern by which the marriage is governed, a division of responsibilities. Without some rules of the road, a marriage would be chaotic—as some are! This role structure, however, seems "radical." It seems to smack of patriarchalism, of an age long gone. What Dark Ages dogma is this that appears to give husbands *carte blanche* and wives a put-down? Sure enough, husbands have read it to boast, wives to bristle. And a growing number of Christian feminists argue a rationale that assigns different meanings to the key words *head* and *subject*. Their interpretation repudiates the whole concept of marital hierarchy. But is this not a misunderstanding, perhaps born of overreaction? It is at least understandable in light of the way male chauvinism has so often dominated Christian circles. But may we not suppose, rather, that *the Divine Author of marriage has an order for its continuing welfare,* a role structure of His own appointing—that He knows best what roles are suited to each spouse, and that His mandate has greater relevance than we give it credit for? Let us begin with the passage itself:

Be subject to one another out of reverence for Christ. Wives, be subject to your husbands, as to the Lord. For the husband is the head of the wife as Christ is the head of the church, his body, and is himself its Savior. As the church is subject to Christ, so let wives also be subject in everything to their husbands. Husbands, love your wives, as Christ loved the church and gave himself up for her, that he might sanctify her, having cleansed her by the washing of water with the word, that he might present the church to himself in splendor, without spot or wrinkle or any such thing, that she might be holy and without blemish. Even so husbands should love their wives as their own bodies. He who loves his wife loves himself. For no man ever hates his own flesh, but nourishes and cherishes it, as Christ does the church, because we are members of his body. "For this reason a man shall leave his father and mother and be joined to his wife, and the two shall become one." This is a great mystery, and I take it to mean Christ and the church; however, let each one of you love his wife as himself, and let the wife see that she respects her husband (Eph. 5:21–33).

Hierarchy of Marital Positions

We can neither avoid nor deny that Ephesians 5:21–33 sets forth a hierarchy of marital positions. The husband is appointed "head," standing over his wife with responsibility and commensurate authority to carry out that responsibility. The wife is to be "in submission" to her husband (and the word means "to stand under"). Now, if we seriously speak of equal-partnership marriage—and we do—how is this hierarchy of positions compatible with equality?[2] *It sounds like the husband is more equal than his wife!* But at the heart of the matter there is a paradox, beautiful when fully understood, even more beautiful when put into practice. In some respects, marriage is an equal partnership, in other respects an unequal one. In its practical outworking there is a superior equality to which both partners' roles make their unique contribution. This is the paradox of it all.

Verse 21 calls for each partner to defer to the other, to be in subjection to the other. This in no wise contradicts the concept of headship and the special subjection of the wife that makes headship possible. For verse 22 immediately goes on (in the Greek it continues the same sentence) to set forth the husband's headship and the wife's special subjection to it. What this says puts us on notice that headship and subjection under God actually work to the end that the beautiful outcome is mutual subjection and loving servanthood. This we must keep in mind as we work our way through the biblical concept; there is a mutuality throughout. Otherwise, should a couple not have a trusting relationship to Christ, a mutual subjection to Him, any attempted headship and its

2. For a full exposition of this subject see the author's book *Marriage as Equal Partnership* (Grand Rapids, MI: Baker, 1980).

corresponding subjection would only result in an unequal, oppressive relationship. Christ must be the governing Center. *There must be submission to Him on the part of both.*

The problem seems to focus on the hierarchy of roles and what we are conditioned to suspect of any human hierarchy, that it will be unjust and result in inequality. Yet, in every social institution known to man, there is a governing structure with its hierarchy of positions. When improperly employed, this of course can be exploitative and destructive of social good. But when properly employed, it can bring a smooth-working order and harmony. *Unequal positions do not necessarily lead to unequal dignity or unequal benefits.* To think otherwise is an incorrect assumption and does not apply to Christian marriage roles.

Nothing in the passage indicates that the roles of husband and wife are ever reversed or rescinded. They are not interchangeable. This rests on the fact that the analogy is drawn from an unchanging relationship—that between Christ and the church. The husband stands in relation to his wife as Christ stands in relation to His church; the wife stands in relation to her husband as the church stands in relation to Christ. The analogy is Christological and thus not subject to change. It does not find its source in culture, contrary to the claims of some. We are not permitted at this point to say that Paul was conditioned by the cultural patterns of his day. It is a spiritual analogy.

How Is Equality Achieved?

In the paradox of an unequal yet equal marriage, there has to be an operational element that transforms inequality of position into equality of dignity and marital benefits. By what means is this accomplished? Here lies the key to it all.

Husbands are commanded to love their wives as Christ loved the church and gave Himself up for her. Love made Him subject to her deepest needs, beginning with the need for redemption at the cost of His blood. Love made Him willing to give Himself to the utmost in order to fulfill those needs completely. Through the same quality of love, the husband-head is subject to his wife and her needs. As head, the husband is subject to Christ in a very special way. Under Christ's headship, the husband exercises his own headship as directed. The husband's is no independent, self-willed, or self-directed headship. This forever precludes his being boss, tyrant, or in any manner an authoritarian who domineeringly lords it over his wife. Headship allows for no self-assertiveness in that role. The husband cannot make arbitrary demands, cannot assume any greater prerogatives of wisdom, power, personal place, or whatever. *He is head only insofar as he himself is subject to his sovereign and governing Head, Jesus Christ the Lord.*

What headship means in a positive sense is that the husband carries responsibility for the welfare and progress of the marriage as God Himself directs. The husband is responsible for a full-partnership marriage in which the potential of both partners finds full opportunity. In this manner, headship "over" is transformed into headship "on behalf of." To be head is actually to be servant, to lead through love. What an amazingly unique concept this is!

Leading Through Loving

Briefly but importantly, what is the nature of agape love as modeled by our Lord Jesus Christ?[3] The agape love of Jesus is never domineering or manipulative, never seeks its own interests either primarily or exclusively, never takes advantage, never puts down another in proud condescension, never seeks to control or suppress. Instead, agape love facilitates the growth and self-realization of another. Love puts the other's needs and potential foremost, accepting the other's opinions, tastes, and choices as worthy of full and respectful consideration. Love affirms the creative possibili-

3. For a full exposition of this theme, see the later chapters in the author's book *How Shall I Love You?* (New York: Harper & Row, 1979). Also see Lewis B. Smedes, *Love Within Limits: A Realist's View of I Corinthians 13* (Grand Rapids: Wm. B. Eerdmans, 1978).

ties of another, though never in a patronizing manner. Love delights to encourage, to stimulate resourcefulness, then to praise the efforts, however deficient they may seem. Love accepts responsibility yet delegates wherever fitting. Love protects the other from whatever would harm or impede the rise to full personhood. Love takes risks, willingly becomes vulnerable wherever necessary, makes whatever sacrifice is required for the other's good. In a word, loving is full-service caring. This is the model of headship we have in Christ, and this is the way—the only way—that a husband's headship in marriage will work successfully and happily! Is there a Christian wife anywhere who would not willingly and joyfully be subject to such love?

Jesus as Subject Servant

The special subjection of the wife does not call her to take an inferior place or role. It does not ask her to be a diminished person in any way. It places her, rather, in a harmonious relationship to her husband's appointed responsibility and love-leadership. Her model of subjection, like her husband's model of headship, is Jesus—the loving Servant-Lord. He is the model of the selfless person who lovingly serves from the position of humility and self-sacrifice. Paul tells us that Christ took the form of a servant (Phil. 2:7). Jesus Himself said that he who would be greatest shall be servant of all (Mark 10:43–44). Thus the husband takes the model of Jesus the Head, and the wife takes the model of Jesus the Servant. But it is the same Jesus—loving Servant! Although each spouse starts from a distinct and separate role, the outcome is mutual, reciprocal, Christlike loving servanthood. The personal individuality and dignity of each spouse is maintained while the gifts of both are utilized to the fullest. Subjection, having its source and model in Jesus, is not self-defeating but self-fulfilling in the highest sense. This is the very glory of the paradox!

For either partner to fulfill his or her appointed role requires nothing less than the empowering of the Holy Spirit.

To model Jesus in any respect is not a human feat. In this sense, Christian marriage is not a human feat. We have a major task ahead, especially in our teaching ministry. This is to teach young people that Christian marriage involves a superhuman role structure and superhuman enablement. This enablement is theirs for the seeking—in Christ. Christian marriage can therefore not be a successful venture if left only to the resourcefulness of sincere Christian young people; their marriage must be kept under the lordship of Jesus Christ. In Him they must find the role model, the daily direction, and the enabling power. Only by this course can the disintegrating forces of modern life that lead toward marital breakup be lessened or precluded altogether.

Is it not fascinating to note that Scripture goes no further in setting forth husband-wife roles? There are no detailed descriptions or illustrations of how these roles are to be carried out in daily living. Only the principles are given us. But these are sufficient for success, sufficient to speak to the diversity of cultural norms represented by so many different countries and covering so many different centuries in the church's history. The principles are unchanging. And it is the same God who strengthens and guides us into His best.

Do We Meet God's Standard?

A minimum of reflection leads to one conclusion: *Not all marriages among professing Christians are Christian marriages*. We cannot say of all, "whom God has joined together." They do not all meet the standard God sets; they are not all covenants of unity and fidelity representative of Christ and His church. They do not all follow the role structure laid down in Scripture. Nor do they all look to God for His empowering for their success. In fact, many are merely Christian in name only.

An even more fundamental question might be asked: "Are both spouses committed to Jesus Christ as Lord?" It is not enough just to acknowledge Jesus as one's Savior. Is He Lord of their life, Lord of their marriage? Are they striving to be obedient to His will? Are they fortified as a couple by their Christian commitment against forces without and within that could possibly destroy their marriage? If not, then somewhere down the line breakup and dissolution may be inevitable. If their resources for success are no more than what they themselves bring to the union, they are not headed down the road to success.

Covenant Faithlessness— Cause for Divorce

In light of our study of the covenant basis for Christian marriage, a question of great suggestiveness arises. This is a question that can be answered only suggestively, not dogmatically. But it is a question that vastly enlarges the issue of marriage and divorce among Christians, especially in our day.

We have considered the nature of covenant faithlessness in its manifold dimensions. The most blatant violation of covenant fidelity is an overt physical act that strikes at the very heart of an exclusive commitment—the act of adultery. Jesus Himself said this was cause for divorce. As we shall see later, this exception allowing divorce was made in the context of a debate that focused on Mosaic legislation. But adultery is only the most blatant way to violate the covenant. The Jews had no clear concept of marriage as representative of God's covenant unity with His people. This sacred symbol is spelled out in the New Testament Letter to the Ephesians. Christians now have a clear and decidedly higher standard of what marriage represents, and also of what kind of violations breach that representation. It is for this reason that we are led to ask if covenant infidelity may well include other violations besides the sexual. Are there other forms of faithlessness besides adultery? We are inclined to say *yes*. For to repudiate covenant unity and its obligations—to no longer regard one's marriage as representative of the permanent, exclusive, loving covenant between Christ and His church—is to break the covenant just as surely as sexual unfaithfulness breaks that covenant. This concept is being increasingly examined.

The reasoning that supports this view is, to say the least, sound theological thinking. And it speaks in a satisfying way to an otherwise unresolved question. Jesus said that apart from the one exception, to divorce is to commit adultery against one's spouse. But actual adultery may not be involved at all. In what sense, then, does the term *adultery* apply? In later chapters we shall use the term *ethical adultery*. Briefly for now, let us put this in the context of a covenant of unity and fidelity.

"Adultery," the term used repeatedly in the Old Testament to speak of Israel's faithlessness to her covenant relationship with God, is used in the same way by Jesus. When the Pharisees asked to see a sign, Jesus replied, "An evil and adulterous generation seeks for a sign . . ." (Matt. 16:4). He was not speaking, of course, of sinful sexual practices in Israel, but of spiritual adultery, spiritual unfaithfulness. However narrowly or broadly Jesus might allow the term *adultery* to refer to sins that destroy the marriage covenant (*porneia* is a broad term, as we shall see), Scripture uses "adultery" to mean covenant faithlessness.

Understanding marriage within this comprehensive framework of covenant, might Jesus say that divorce is not inherently justified except as one partner is unfaithful to the covenant of unity and fidelity? Might He then rephrase to say, "And to divorce and marry another is to break your covenant of permanence and exclusivity, which represents Christ and His church"? In support of this possibility, we note that it harmonizes the meaning of divorce with the deeper meanings of marriage. It is certainly a conceptual necessity that if we have developed a more adequate New Testament view of marriage, we need to complement it with a more adequate view of what marital dissolution dissolves, what divorce divorces. To thoughtful Christians today, it is meaningful to believe that anything that thoroughly destroys and repudiates the marriage covenant of unity and fidelity as defined in Scripture is infidelity, and hence a legitimate cause for divorce.

From our examination of what it means to break the marriage covenant of unity and fidelity—sometimes seriously enough to justify divorce—we can list only one scriptural illustration. Jesus pointed to adultery, faithlessness to the exclusive sexual bond constitutive of marriage. We have seen that an extended study of what the covenant relationship involves indicates that other violations—or outright repudiation—may be equally destructive of covenant integrity. However we may understand this complex question of cause, we are only talking about the truly serious—the true covenant-breaking conditions that can arise. To divorce for purely selfish motives—to indulge a new love, to be free from burdening responsibilities, to end some bitter dispute—such reasons are not justifiable. Marriage is serious business in the sight of God, and only extreme, unresolvable, covenant-breaking conditions should be allowed to justify divorce.

We close on a more promising note, with an additional truth from within the covenant concept: *As covenants can be broken, so can they be renewed as well.* Any sin against marriage can be forgiven, any covenant violation reconciled, any covenant-breaker restored—that is, if the partner at fault is repentant and the other partner willing to forgive. God is honored whenever the forgiving love of the Lord Jesus Christ is exemplified by a forgiving spouse. Even as we renew our covenant with God from time to time, consecrating our life to Him anew, so husbands and wives need to renew their covenant consecration to each other. We need constant reminders of that to which we have committed ourselves—the mutual loving servanthood, the covenant obligations—all that keeps marriage alive and growing.

It is one thing to know that if marriage fails and divorce follows, God will meet us in grace. It is the better thing to seek to establish a Christian marriage that is impervious to the forces that can disrupt and destroy marriage.

3

Grace Transcendent, Grace Triumphant!

At one of our regional pastors' seminars, a concerned minister, evidently fearful lest an emphasis upon grace result in diminishing the force of his pulpit exhortations, said, "Professor Small, aren't you opening the door to divorce?" My reply was: "Not so; *that* door's already open. I'm seeking to open the door to God's forgiving, renewing grace. *That* door still hasn't been opened as it should!"

Abusing the Truth

It is worthy of at least a comment or two to observe that any and all truth is subject to abuse by anyone bent on abusing it. Take, for example, 1 John 1:9. How often I have turned to this Scripture in starting a new believer on the Christian walk. How reassuring to know that "If we confess our sins, he is faithful and just, and will forgive our sins and cleanse us from all unrighteousness." What then? Is the new Christian likely to say, "Oh, I'm glad to hear this! Now I know I can sin without having to worry about it, because I can just confess it and be forgiven. If it weren't for that, I might be too concerned about sinning."

Too concerned about sinning! Really? If someone made

63

that reply, would we not lovingly but surely help him to see how deeply faulty is his thinking, how false to the mind and character of God? The answer to this from Scripture is Romans 6:1–2: "What shall we say then? Are we to continue in sin that grace may abound? By no means! How can we who died to sin still live in it?" Paul then goes on to explain how our union with Christ is designed to free us from sin and make us "slaves of righteousness" (v. 18). *Forgiveness should motivate us to righteous living.*

It is quite understandable that in a day of irresponsible and hasty marriage, easy divorce, and all the temptations assailing even the most mature Christian couples, we must avoid any semblance of encouraging marital breakup. I have been professionally engaged for over thirty years in teaching and publishing, traveling to distant seminars and conferences, all to the end that I might be a teacher-strengthener of Christian marriages. This was my special course for twelve years on the faculty of Westmont College, and I have published six books on Christian-marriage themes. Yet, in all honesty I must concern myself just as seriously with the tragedy of divorce and the hopefulness of remarriage. I must not shrink back, fearing that a view other than legalism may be new and suspect to some evangelical brethren. We know how they, as I, were taught a legalistic, judgmental approach in a day when divorce was uncommon in our congregations, and all we could see was the evil of divorce and not the plight of actual persons. Then we could afford to gather our robes around ourselves, as it were, and keep aloof from the problem. But no longer! And my great encouragement over the past ten years since first I wrote on the grace aspects of this subject is to see hundreds upon hundreds of pastors set free within the larger perspective of God's present governance by grace—perfect righteousness mediated in times of failure by grace. May the trend continue. The church has been badly in need of healthier attitudes and a more positive ethic. Happily, the state of things is looking up!

God's Extraordinary Ideal

If anything is assimilated from the studies ahead, may it be that the rule of grace does not place Christian couples under a new law, but under an extraordinary ideal—an ideal framed by the perfect intention God had for marriage from the beginning. Our aim is clear—to fulfill the perfect ideal given to guide us in doing His will and experiencing His best. So far as we are able, the marriage ideal is to be fulfilled with the Spirit's empowerment. Another purpose served by the marriage ideal is that it puts marriage under divine judgment; the ideal is the standard by which marriage is judged. However, failure to meet the ideal does not place one under penalty or beyond God's forgiveness and renewing power. Even a broken ideal is rich with hope, for in God's renewing grace we return to the ideal. In either a restored relationship or a new relationship altogether, we can seek once again to achieve that ideal.

If the church chooses to feel embarrassment over its members' conduct, let it choose more likely targets than the divorced. Why not the inveterate gossip, say, or the proud self-righteous officeholder, or perhaps the Christian of questionable morals? Have not the divorced borne the office of scapegoat long enough? The embarrassment is that the church cannot minister adequately to people it holds under judgment, or when its theology goes no further than legalism and narrow exposition of God's Word. God opens the doors to ministry and we close them. Unwilling to face the complex needs of the divorced, the church often subtly turns them away. So often the attitude has been, "We're sorry, but you made your bed; now you must lie in it. You made a horrible mistake, and we can't encourage you to make another in remarrying. After all, two wrongs cannot make a right. You will just have to endure the consequences and ask the Lord to give you grace to suffer it." Pathetic indeed to suppose that this attitude could ever represent the God of grace!

If it were not divorce, "only" murder, say, and the guilty

one had spent his time in prison and had been converted while there, how eager we would be to book his testimony! Most likely he would become a Christian celebrity and travel from church to church. (Hopefully, ours could get him first!) But woe unto that person if he were divorced! "Well," we say, "that's different, you know. Such a person would be a bad model in our congregation, might have a bad influence on the young."

Now, really, let's be sensible. A divorced person might be just the very one whom God could use to go to others in marital difficulty to explain the pain and loss incurred by divorce, to tell of the damaging factors not usually considered when one is hurting and bent on divorce. Is this not the very person who could put arms around another presently going through divorce, comforting, encouraging, or just sharing the hurt? Is this not the person who could describe the healing ministry of God to those whose lives have been broken by divorce? Is there anyone in better position to witness to God's forgiving, renewing grace? Is this not the person best equipped to put together a support group in a church that truly has the marks of caring love?

Churches that have no ministry to the divorced are to that extent diminished in their potential for God and His people. Thank God for those churches with sharing and support groups, who invite the divorced into a special fellowship, who actively place hurting ones with people who care because they themselves know what healing is all about. And thrice shame upon those churches that are too self-righteous and rigid to welcome the divorced!

There is an uneasy conscience in the church today, and rightly so. This surfaces in every pastors' conference I have conducted over the past fifteen years or so. Surely the God of compassion is speaking. Have we ears to hear and hearts to respond? Or are we content to be evangelical Pharisees?

The Sin of
Falsely Contrived Judgments

One of the major teachers of the "no divorce, no re-marriage, no exception" school deftly employs a fear tactic by suggesting a number of serious consequences that he claims will inevitably come upon any person who divorces and remarries. No matter what the cause or circumstance, every divorced-remarried person faces the same conse-quences. From one illustrated case, the same consequences are applied to all cases. The state of every divorced-remarried person is thus made untenable. In published ma-terials that thousands have studied, a question is asked: "Why do people in the church tend to shun the remarried?" (Note the assumption that this is invariably the case.) The proposed reason is based on Proverbs 6:29–35, essentially the words suggesting reproach to one's name. Let us ex-amine this briefly.

We need only read the entire passage to see that it is not speaking about a person who has divorced and remarried, but about a person who has committed adultery! And what is the intended message? The *adulterer* will get "wounds and dishonor," and "his disgrace will not be wiped away. For [note the reason carefully] *jealousy makes a man furious, and he will not spare when he takes revenge*" (vv. 33–34, italics added). Now, I ask you, what does this have to do with the reputation of a remarried person or why such a person is shunned in the church? This view, widespread in our coun-try, teaches further that this will be one of the more promi-nent and continuing consequences for remarrying, and that this reproach will diminish the individual's effectiveness. Who says all this? Not God in His Word, only the anti-divorce teacher who contrived it with a misuse of Scripture.

Now, to be sure, at times God appoints negative temporal consequences. Many divorced suffer from wrong choices and wrong actions. God may want some dear lessons to be learned, perhaps also as a witness to the tragedy of divorce.

But this is not inevitably the case for everyone. One of the wonders of Christian experience is that God so often wipes out all temporal consequences in a special measure of His goodness, often directly turning ill to good. We simply cannot limit God by our little concepts of what He must do in given situations because this is what seems right to us. We cannot make *our* judgment out to be *God's* or suggest the consequences *we* think should follow. God always shows Himself bigger than the little boxes we create for Him. Only He knows what consequences should follow all our actions.

When this anti-divorce teaching raises the question of why the church tends to shun the remarried (although not as often as the teacher supposes), the answer, sadly enough, has less to do with the person being shunned than with the sin of the congregation that does the shunning! (For further critique of this popular teaching, see Appendix C.)

Code-Book Ethics Found Wanting

This seems as appropriate a place as any for a digression. It is interesting to observe that those having the greatest difficulty accepting grace ethics are often those who prefer their ethics to be absolute and authority-oriented, with either compliance or judgment the only possible outcomes. For them the Bible is most comfortably a code book of black-and-white rules. Answers to ethical questions are always *yes* or *no*. Every issue divides simply into "either-or." One course of action is right, all others wrong. We might refer to this as "pigeonhole ethics." It has the advantage that one can always be sure of the answer, for there is only one answer. Answers can be readily proof-texted, stopping further examination. It is never as though a certain act may have different consequences in different circumstances, may be motivated by a variety of reasons, and thus may be right under one set of circumstances and wrong in another. No—to such thinking, this unnecessarily introduces an element of ambiguity. Some people prefer dogma to debate, seeking simple answers to complex problems. To suggest that some ethical choices are (God forbid!) "situational" is more than some people can handle. No, they say, we must be perfectly consistent in "Thus saith the Lord." We dare not ever say, "I don't know the mind of the Lord on this matter." With such thinking, any indecisiveness is tantamount to compromise or unbelief, to moral vacillation. Ethical choices are to be clear-cut, never matters of pastoral discretion after much study and prayer. Nothing, absolutely nothing, must deter us from being able to teach "ten reasons why these consequences will always follow." We must gird up our loins and flatly tell God's waiting people that there are no questions, no doubts as to how God will act in every situation. As His law is unchanging, so also is its application—*World without end. Amen!*

Ah, yes, how much easier for us all if only this *were* the case! We would only need fill our notebook with wisdom handed down from some spiritual guru, memorize the stock answers in the manual, and everything would fall into place and our minds would be at rest. No need for prolonged, thoughtful wrestling with issues, no need to search out a balance between competing ethical interests, no need to determine if a course of action thought to be correct has unacceptable costs or unresolved questions. No need to wrestle with which of two possible courses of action would minimize human suffering and maximize human potential. Nor would we have to make responsible choices at all; they would all be made for us by our code book. We could rest content with abstract, universal ethical rules, never having a worry whether or not they fit actual situations. Neither would the dignity and well-being of individuals be a legitimate concern. Just give us a set of rules clearly spelled out; we need nothing more. Then we can get on with building *The Church of Accomplished Sainthood* (thanking God, of course, that we have learned the Ten Steps to Sainthood).

Yes, would that it were so! Would that the world were so simple and uncomplicated. Yes, would that we were not ensconced in a fallen world. Then we would not be embarrassed by having divorced people in the church; we could wipe out that option and bask in our righteousness. But enough of this digression. Surely the point has been made:

Beware of easy solutions to complex problems! Don't force the Bible into easy answers! Be wary of those who assure you they have all the answers. Yes, be wary of books; not every expert writes books, and not every book is written by an expert! So, be wary of this book, too. Don't swallow it—book, line, and thinker! One writer's conclusions may be helpful, but none can be final. The intelligent reader will consult books of different persuasions. But most of all we need the ministry of the Holy Spirit to guide us through the maze of competing interpretations. Use *this* book as one source only.

The Nature of Ideals

For the church of the interim age, we have lifted the saying of Jesus about divorce and remarriage from the place of "law" to that of "ideal." This calls for some examination. An ideal is non-exceptional; that is, it is true and correct and not subject to any exceptions. *An ideal is just as absolute as divine law, yet it looks to different possibilities in terms of its fulfillment.* There are degrees of success and failure in the attainment of an ideal; this is not true of law. How different are the two! When an ideal is not attained, it can be reinstated; one can try again. When a law is violated, it incurs penalty. The violator is not given the opportunity to try again. Laws carry sanctions, but ideals do not. If the saying of Jesus were indeed law, then violation of it would entail sanctions. Our legalistic friends would be right after all—there would be serious consequences imposed by God. Of course, we would expect God in faithfulness to warn us of these consequences. Interestingly, He does not.

If God's absolute intention is set before the church as an ideal, the consequence of failure to attain the ideal is not penalty; rather, it calls forth God's redemptive action. Opportunity is afforded by His forgiving grace to seek once more to regain the ideal and fulfill it in another attempt. It might be the restoration of a broken marriage in a successful new beginning. Failing that, it might be through the pain and devastation of divorce, leading at last to a remarriage in which the ideal is fulfilled.

Jesus insisted upon the *ideal* of marriage. It alone will bring lasting happiness and the fulfillment of God's creative intent. Even in changing times, this ideal is not subject to change. But as the church developed, new problems arose, and the church found it necessary to deal with them in ways that neither Jesus nor Paul touched upon. This process goes on today. One of the most difficult aspects in arriving at a satisfactory interpretation of all the data is in the realm of decisions that pastors make in their day-by-day ministry.

A Common Pastoral Dilemma

One of the questions asked repeatedly in pastors' seminars is usually put this way: "When I'm asked to officiate at a marriage where there has been a previous divorce, I wonder about my role. I represent the church, and it's my understanding that unless there is a biblical cause for divorce, I am participating in an act which is sinful. Is this not complicity in the guilt?" This is a difficult question for many a godly pastor. Let me address this here as I do in the seminars:

Whatever we say about the couple's marrying after divorce is just what we say about the pastor who marries them. His participation *does* involve complicity in what they are doing. But is it sinful for him to do so?

If we say that the couple has a right to remarry, what kind of right do we mean? Surely not personal right, not a right inherent in the orders of creation, nor in kingdom law. *Properly, it is not a right at all, but a privilege granted in God's provisional will.* But because all remarriage after divorce involves a breach of God's original design, it involves human sin as well. Although it may not involve willful sin or necessarily sin against a person, it is nonetheless sin against God's purpose in marriage, against His unconditional will. Yet it is forgivable sin for the penitent who applies for God's forgiving grace. God in turn is free to bless the penitent with the healing of a new marriage. Surely God delights in the normalization of married life with its full family reestablishment, especially when the center of the relationship is commitment to His Son.

Now, having reviewed this, retrace these steps as they relate to the officiating pastor. God has stood in judgment upon the breach of His will; this the couple acknowledges. But then God takes another stand, now as the God of all grace. This is, as it were, a second phase. The pastor first acknowledges together with the marrying couple that sin was present in the divorce action, whatever the cause, whatever one's "innocence." The pastor discharges his responsibility as God's representative in this first phase. Then, like God Himself, the pastor moves on to the second phase and now represents the God of all grace. He can affirm God's forgiveness and proceed to complete the ceremony, pronouncing God's blessing upon the new union. As part of that ceremony, he will require the couple to commit themselves to so live as to faithfully fulfill God's design for a covenant of unity and fidelity. And so it is that the officiating pastor stands as God's representative *first* in terms of God's judgment and *second* in terms of God's grace. It is not a contradiction that the officiating pastor thus takes a dual role, the one preparing for the other.

Sometimes Sin, Always Failure

Let us be precise about one thing: *All divorce is failure, and failure itself represents a breach of God's intent.* God judges this to be sinful. However, this does not mean that divorce is always a direct result of sin on the part of one or both partners. In some instances it is, but not always. Yet of every divorce it can be said that it is a consequence of the disorder brought into our world by sin. That disorder may be present from the very beginning of a relationship. Unforeseen disabling factors may actually have been present before a pair married. The resulting mismatch becomes overwhelming if the individuals simply are incapable of overcoming their disability sufficiently to live together as man and wife with a modicum of success. Dissolution, then, may have been written into the relationship from the very start. But here we must be careful in our judgment; human weakness or the tendency toward mistaken action is not "sin." Thus all divorce is not the consequence of either particular sin or hardness of heart. Sometimes divorce signifies the sad truth that a marriage was not a true marriage by any scriptural or rational index. The failure in such instances is not the divorce but the marriage. Divorce brings that failure to its final resolution. There is a subtle if sad truth in the one-liner, "Marriage is the cause of divorce." Sometimes the perpetuation of marriage is the perpetuation of a mistake. Can God reverse such failures? In many instances, yes. Does He choose to do so in every instance? No. We who are not privy to His purposes cannot lay claim to know His mind and will.

Grace Plus Nothing

There is one misunderstanding of grace that merits brief mention, only because some popular materials now in circulation suggest that God works out His compassion toward the divorced on a principle of "tolerance." Nothing could be further from the truth! Tolerance, like leniency, precludes the operation of grace altogether, as Paul Tournier carefully points out. Tolerance or leniency is a way of overlooking the true nature of an offense, as though it were not really serious in God's eyes; God merely shrugs His shoulders and turns the other way. But divorce *is* a serious matter that cannot be glossed over by tolerance or leniency! For one thing, it precludes God's revealing the true tragedy of violating His design and the costly grace that is His response. And, too, the sin needs to be confessed and forgiven—not merely tolerated. God is hurt when we breach His purpose for marriage, and we owe Him our heartfelt penitence. We recognize that—whatever our sin—God does not tolerate it. Rather, His nature is to *bear* our sins and failures and to redeem us at cost to Himself. The notion of tolerance cheapens the nature of grace. God acts toward us in the highest possibilities of divine love, and the single principle at work is His free grace.

We are by nature so tuned to the notion of justice, to the idea that a person must get his just deserts, that we find it most difficult at times to accept the revelation of God's grace. But whatever failure we bring to Him, the principle upon which He acts is the same; *it is grace plus nothing!*

Remarriage As Healing Grace

For some persons, not all by any means, remarriage is a redemptive fulfillment, a new opportunity to reverse the former failure, to seek an enduring Christ-honoring marriage, and to fulfill the orders of creation. Where divorce has been deemed necessary for the welfare of one or both parties, divorced persons may enter new marriages so centered in Christ's purpose and love that any dissolution of these marriages would be most unlikely. The tragedy of the former marriage that ended may greatly deepen the understanding and resolve of the remarrying person as to what a Christian marriage truly is. Pastors across the land bear witness to such remarriages, rich with understanding and commitment.

Dr. Ray Anderson of Fuller Theological Seminary, an esteemed former colleague whose insights have distilled into my own, says it so well: "If the church is such a thing as grace, then let the church be bold in grace! The stigmas that the church places upon those who bear the marks of sin have no existence in the sight of Christ." Yes, having been admitted to the church of grace, let us be bold in that grace! That is the plea of this book—Let the church be bold in grace! Let the divorced and remarried feel fully accepted in the community of sinners saved by grace, for we are sinners all. Be reminded once more that grace is God's freely given, unmerited favor toward us, the expression of His unconditional, redemptive love.

Set the remarried free to find their place of service in the church, alongside those whose experience of the forgiving grace of God may have been in less conspicuous areas of life's struggle. Let there be no penalties in the church when God has disallowed such penalties. May there be no distinctions in the body of Christ based on color, sex, or marital status. In instances of divorce, let there be full recognition of the necessity at times of choosing the lesser of two evils as the only possible remaining good. Let us rejoice that the absolute will of God in all its beauty and perfection cannot be compromised, but that He administers His will toward us in His grace-response to our imperfect faith and obedience, our sin and our failure. May the knowledge of such grace fill our hearts with responding love such as will motivate us in every way to seek His highest and best. May no man rob us of this! This is God's last and best word to us!

So Let's Move On

In this introductory part of the book, sufficient has been set forth to indicate our major thesis: God's renewing grace. A "theology of grace" leads invariably to an "ethic of grace." It is grace that is to govern all our considerations. Where New Testament interpretation of the problem of divorce and remarriage may require our choosing the direction of either law or grace, our governing theological ethic demands going in the direction of grace. Either the New Testament presents a governing ethic of grace, or it does not. If the grace principle is true, and if it governs every ethical problem that Christians face in their personal lives, then it must be applied consistently. Our study of divorce and remarriage seeks above all else to be consistent with this governing ethic of grace.

Having stated our thesis, it remains to work this out in two aspects. Part II will take up the biblical materials, both Old and New Testament texts, letting God speak directly in the whole counsel of His Word. Part III will set forth the larger ethical framework within which God has chosen to govern His people throughout the different ages of redemption, focusing upon the ruling ethic that governs the church age of which we are a part. This somewhat complex subject is integral to our study as a whole, although it is strangely the missing part in most divorce-and-remarriage studies. As we shall discover, a veritable network of ideas comes before us in the study of God's ethical governance, all of which impinge upon the main question. Really, not until Part Three is in place can the thesis of the book be judged to be correct or incorrect. So now let us move directly to the biblical materials that are the foundation of all that follows.

PART TWO

The Specific Biblical Teachings on Divorce and Remarriage

4

Old Testament Provision

Quite naturally we turn first to the Old Testament for the origins of biblical teaching on divorce and remarriage. Although it does not give us teaching upon which we can build a *Christian* perspective, it does give us insight of a special character as to the way God exercises His conditional, or provisional, will. Here we meet God administering His will in the form of absolute law, the Mosaic law. Even in the midst of a legal system with severe penalties for failure to obey the law, we find a divine concession to man's weakness and failure with reference to marriage. Contrary to our expectations regarding inflexible law, divorce and remarriage are both permitted.

What teaching we find in the Old Testament is curiously meager, somewhat obscure, and largely incidental. There is no systematic teaching on the subject; it seems virtually of no concern to the Old Testament to pursue at length the themes of monogamous marriage, marital disruption and divorce, or the consequences of remarriage. The *Encyclopedia Judaica* says that divorce and remarriage were accepted as an established custom in ancient Israel.

That assumption clearly lies behind the few references in the New Testament. The subject of divorce really does not appear at all until Mosaic legislation is enacted. In fact, there is no marriage law as such, so there can be no contra-

79

vening of marriage law by divorce law. Marriage is not set in legal or contractual terms, but rather is based on a principle noted at the very first union of man and woman. Immediately following the account of the creation of Eve and her union with Adam, we read in Genesis 2:24: "Therefore a man leaves his father and his mother and cleaves to his wife, and they become one flesh." Creation orders are suited to mankind before the fall. *There marriage was designed to be indissoluble, an enduring relationship through life.* A growing couple-unity was to characterize marriage so as to make it a total union in which both husband and wife were completed by the other. Life became an integrated whole whenever a man and a woman were permanently united. Marriage was an organic whole of which the two persons were equal complementary halves.

Without the forces of evil to disrupt this union, Adam and Eve represented the ideal of marriage without possibility of divorce. *No provision for divorce and remarriage was made in the orders of creation.* It is to this that Jesus referred in Matthew 19:8, ". . . but from the beginning it was not so." He pointed to God's original purpose, an intention that had not changed in His time and has not changed in ours. No divorce or remarriage had been programmed for mankind's marital experience under the conditions of original sinlessness. Only the disruption and disorder of a fallen world could make this a possible and necessary option. The rupture of this divinely instituted human bond is conceivable only if first of all there is a rupture in the divine-human relationship. At the very outset this defines the nature and basis of marriage and clearly implies that no dissolution of the marriage bond could be contemplated except as a radical breach of the divine institution. It is an aberration of the will of God. It was impossible to envision marital dissolution as anything other than abnormal and evil. Such was the ethical context of "the beginning," when as yet mankind was free from the thralldom and disintegrating power of sin.

With the entrance of sin came a new complex of condi-

tions and circumstances. Since sin desecrates all relationships, we face the question of the bearing of sin upon the
sanctity of marriage. With failure and disruption per-
meating *all* human relationships, it was inevitable that
such failure would manifest itself in the most intimate
and demanding of life's personal relationships—marriage.
Granting the original principle of the indissolubility of the
marriage bond, we ask, "Are there now, by reason of sin,
conditions under which marriage may be dissolved with divine sanction?" Can we say with Lewis Smedes, "This is not
to say that God approves of divorce; it is only to say that he
sometimes disapproves of its alternatives even more than
he disapproves of divorce"? Again, shall we be able to say
with Smedes, "But with all his laws, he accommodates specific intentions to his deepest and most general intention:
the well-being of his children. To that end, one act that is
generally conceded to be an evil is morally permitted if it is
necessary to avoid a greater evil."? In other words, shall the
intention of God be accommodated to the necessities of
man's weakness and failure? John Murray reflects, "It is
quite conceivable that while the reason for divorce is sinful, the right of divorce for that reason may be divine." This
is a profound and highly relevant statement, and this author is in agreement with both Smedes and Murray. Our
study will elaborate on these concepts.

Remarriage Not Prohibited

By the time the nation Israel was organized around
Mosaic law, divorce and remarriage had become customary
practice. Israel was little different from her neighboring nations in this respect. From the Pentateuch we are unable to
discover that God instituted a divorce law. It is also true
that God did not institute a general law prohibiting divorce
or limiting it to one or more specific causes. Now, if divorce
were to be regarded as an absolute prohibition among God's
people Israel, must we not assume that a law of prohibition
would surely have been incorporated within the Mosaic leg-

islation, that the matter would be perfectly clear? But it is not! Instead we have laws restricting some forms of divorce and remarriage. In some cases divorce was forbidden; in other cases it was mandatory. Divorce is always a regrettable necessity, even when it occurs for the best of reasons, but it *does* occur. Law existed only for the reason of regulation. It is interesting to reflect that what God absolutely forbids, He of course does not regulate; this would be self-contradictory.

The bill of divorcement in use in Israel was referred to as "A Bill of Cutting Off." The Hebrew word also means "to put away" and is so translated in some versions. Interestingly, when Joseph suspected Mary of infidelity because she was pregnant and he knew he had not been sexually involved with her, "being a just man and unwilling to put her to shame, [he] resolved to divorce her quietly" (Matt. 1:19). Joseph had this right of private divorce. It was within the law, and was required even though Joseph was not married, only betrothed, to Mary. Call it "betrothal divorce."

The Husband's Divorce Rights

Coming now to Mosaic law as it related to divorce, we refer especially to the studies of David Amram. In the Mosaic law as detailed in Deuteronomy, there were two laws restricting the husband's right to divorce, and one that refers to that right. Deuteronomy 21:10–14 refers to the woman taken captive at war. She may be taken as a wife. If, however, in time the husband finds "no delight in her," he may "let her go where she will" (v. 14). She is privately divorced. Inasmuch as marriage is meant to be indissoluble because two persons are one flesh, it is strange that something as strict as Mosaic law would represent God's intent with relatively easy divorce, as in this case. And there is no mention whatever of divorce disrupting the one-flesh union.

Deuteronomy 22:13–19 has to do with the husband who falsely accuses his wife of prenuptial incontinence. His punishment is that he is deprived of the right of divorce; he is

compelled by law to keep her as his wife forever. Further on
in the same chapter (vv. 28–29) is a second and similar law,
by which punishment is prescribed for the man who rapes a
woman. He must marry her, pay a sum to her father for the
violation of his daughter, and he shall never be permitted to
divorce her all his days. Now this must strike us as strange,
inasmuch as the woman who has been raped may well regard her rapist the last man on earth she wants to be married to—especially for life and without benefit of divorce!
But this was the law of Moses as given by God. Much as we
might deplore the social conditions under which women
lived in those patriarchal times, this was God's appointing.
Our sense of propriety is not always in tune with God's purposes, especially in times remote from our own.

Before these laws were enacted, the husband was under
no restriction whatever; he could divorce his wife whenever
he pleased and for whatever reasons. These laws placed the
first check upon his liberty. *The right of divorce was a private right of husbands alone in this patriarchal system*. The
woman was never entitled to divorce her husband under
Jewish law. Such an act by her would have been in opposi-
tion to the superior rights then granted to husbands over
their wives. Thankfully, this is not in force today!

The Divorced Woman's Status

The legal and social status of the divorced woman is
scarcely touched upon in either the Old or New Testament.
There is nothing to indicate that her position was in any
sense an inferior one; on the contrary, she seems to have en-
joyed certain advantages denied to married women. The divorced woman, like the widow, was her own person. She
could return to her father's house if she liked but was not
under that necessity. Before marriage she was subject to her
father's authority. During marriage her husband was her
master. If widowed or divorced, she did not once again become subject to her father's authority. Rather, she had the
right to give herself in marriage to another, whereas as a

maiden before her maturity, she was given in marriage by her father. Unlike an unmarried woman or a wife, she could bind herself by her own vows to God (Num. 30:9). The only absolute disadvantage that a bill of divorce imposed upon a woman was the denial of her right to marry a priest (Lev. 21:7). Lest it appear from this passage that a divorced woman was classed with bad society, Philo says, "They [the priests] are permitted with impunity to marry not only maidens, but widows also; not indeed all widows, but those whose husbands are dead, for the law thinks it fitting to remove all quarrels and disputes from the life of the priest; and if they have husbands living, there very likely might be disputes from the jealousy which is caused by the love of men for women; but when the first husband is dead, then with him the hostility which could be felt towards the second husband dies also." Although Philo is speaking of women who are "widowed" by divorce, a curious use of the word to us, his point is clear.

The high priest of Israel, by virtue of his exalted and sanctified position, was not permitted to marry a woman other than a virgin, hence neither a widowed or divorced woman (Lev. 21:13–14). In the Prophets especially is found the spiritual symbolism behind this. Israel is spoken of as the one wife of Yahweh. Paul uses the same terminology when he speaks of bringing the Corinthians to Christ: "I betrothed you to Christ to present you as a pure bride to her one husband" (2 Cor. 11:2). Other versions read "pure virgin" or "chaste virgin." The restriction placed upon the high priest goes further than that placed upon the marriage of other priests, for the high priest may not marry a widow. So the widow is put in the same class as the divorced woman in this regard. But note that it is not that divorce downgrades a woman or a priest who marries a divorced woman. Not at all; that is not the point. The whole point is a symbolic one, symbolic of spiritual truth. *The priest is to represent God's intention of being the Husband of a virgin people, a people given to Him alone and to no other*. In other words, this is to speak of an enduring marriage covenant between God and

His people—no disruption, no change in God's bride. Later in the Prophets, Israel is pictured as the unfaithful wife. God separated from her for a season, but His covenant with Israel stands despite her unfaithfulness, and the marriage is reestablished with Israel's repentance.

Divorce was mandatory in the special circumstances confronting Ezra and Nehemiah during the reform movement of their time. (See Ezra 10 and Nehemiah 13.) In Shecaniah's words to Ezra:

> "We have broken faith with our God and have married foreign women from the peoples of the land, but even now there is hope for Israel in spite of this. Therefore let us make a covenant with our God to put away all these wives and their children, according to the counsel of my lord and of those who tremble at the commandment of our God; and let it be done according to the law" (Ezra 10:2–3).

Since God had forbidden marriage with these people, *to divorce these wives was necessary to repudiate their sin.* We shall study a somewhat similar situation in Corinth during Paul's time. Some Christians were married to non-Christians. Divorce there was not mandatory but permitted as a "regulation of necessity," to use the phrase of Helmut Thielicke. We shall see how different is this situation under grace from that under Mosaic law.

A Strange Divine Concession

We turn now to a most important Old Testament text, Deuteronomy 24:1–4—a passage that occupies a unique place in the Old Testament because it contains, as does no other passage, specific legislation bearing upon the question of divorce and remarriage. But to say this is also to point out that it is not a legal text for divorcing; like other texts, it takes divorce for granted. This is to say that legislation very likely did exist, but it was not included in the Pentateuch for some reason. However, this is a legal text, the purpose of which is clearly regulative—one of the major functions of all law. It is not enough to say that it is "a concession." *It is regulative law within the corpus of Mosaic law as given by God.* No better summary statement is available than that of S. R. Driver, "The law is thus not, properly speaking, a law of divorce; the right of divorce is assumed as established by custom . . . but definite formalities are prescribed and restrictions imposed, tending to prevent its being lightly or rashly exercised." This passage in Deuteronomy has special significance because it provides a context of debate that qualifies what Jesus is recorded as saying in the synoptic Gospels. The text reads:

> "When a man takes a wife and marries her, if then she finds no favor in his eyes because he has found some indecency in her, and he writes her a bill of divorce and puts it in her hand and sends her out of his house, and she departs out of his house, and if she goes and becomes another man's wife, and the latter husband dislikes her and writes her a bill of divorce and puts it in her hand and sends her out of his house, or if the latter husband dies, who took her to be his wife, then her former husband, who sent her away, may not take her again to be his wife, after she has been defiled" (Deut. 24:1–4).

This is the only text from Mosaic law that refers in any detail to the termination of marriage by way of divorce. Reuven Yaron points out that nothing in the text in any way expresses disapproval of divorce. It concedes divorce to be the status quo, and no civil or ecclesiastical penalties are attached to it, no social ostracism implied. On the contrary, it gives the wife a legal right to remarry. It aims at preventing hasty divorce on the husband's part. After all, divorce was simple to obtain; there were no court cases, no adversary contest. This required a tempering influence provided by regulative law. Furthermore, Yaron sees this as protective of the second marriage also. When the divorced wife has married another, there is the possibility of tension. The first husband may wish to get his wife back. If she remarried in haste, she, too, may wish to return to her former husband. She may pine for him, fantasizing the possibility of going back to him some day. This would naturally destroy the present marriage; at least it would cause the second husband to suffer jealousy and apprehension. But all such possibilities are precluded by this regulative law. There is no hint of objection to the second marriage, but simply some effective steps given to ensure its stability and continuation. *It makes sure the divorce will stick! It also makes sure the remarriage will stick.* There is no provision for turning back.

The Divorce God Hates

Upon the return of the Israelites from captivity in Babylon, some of them divorced their Jewish wives in order to marry heathen women with whom they had taken up residence and would otherwise have had to leave behind. It was a cruel, wanton forsaking of their wives in favor of these Babylonian women. Against this abuse Malachi raised his voice. Although the law was powerless to prevent this divorcing, morality could not countenance the practice. Malachi says that this is why God will not answer their prayers:

> . . . Because the LORD was witness to the covenant between you and the wife of your youth, to whom you have been faithless, though she is your companion and your wife by covenant. Has not the one God made and sustained for us the spirit of life? And what does he desire? Godly offspring. So take heed to yourselves, and let none be faithless to the wife of his youth. "For I hate divorce," says the LORD the God of Israel . . . (Mal. 2:14–16).

We need caution before generalizing from this account so as to say, "See, God hates each and every divorce that ever occurred. God is against every divorce, whatever the cause." If we can lay aside our bias for a moment and look at the passage in its context, moderation will soon replace this kind of unwarranted generalization.

In general terms I am sure we *can* say of all cases that *God hates* divorce, and so should we. Probably most of us agree that whenever anything in this life is able to break one of God's creative purposes, it is a hateful thing. Whatever hinders the marital plan God has for us is hateful in itself. But, as we shall see as we go on with this study, *nowhere do we find God saying that He hates every divorce for whatever cause.* Nor does He say that He prohibits every divorce for whatever cause. He certainly hates the conditions that bring about divorce. He hates the consequences that attend many divorces, though not all. But if we are going to be fair with Scripture, it is interesting to note that this is the only place God says He hates divorce, and it is unquestionably special hatred for a special kind of divorce. Here is treacherous forsaking of wives for heathen ones. First of all, it is the choice of women outside the covenant of Israel—a thing forbidden. Not only that, it is faithlessness to one's spouse for unjustifiable reasons. To generalize this to cover all instances and causes of divorce, as many do, is totally unwarranted and a twisting of Scripture.

Controversy Divides a Nation

Now, back to our passage in Deuteronomy 24. The crucial yet controversial part of the text has to do with these words: "... she finds no favor in his eyes because he has found some indecency in her . . . and [if] the latter husband dislikes her. . . ." In a legal text, these words would be judged as terribly "ambiguous" as they relate to the husband who first divorced his wife, and downright "trivial" in the succeeding instance. Versions provide little help in even determining what is said, let alone what it means. The King James Version reads "some uncleanness," the New American Standard has "some indecency," while the Jerusalem Bible has "some impropriety," and *The Living Bible* paraphrase, apparently unable to come to anything precise at all, simply says, "If a man doesn't like something about his wife. . . ." The Hebrew literally reads, "because of the nakedness of the matter." Pray tell, what in the world does that mean? It is idiomatic and gives no genuine clue at all. The phrase is variously interpreted in the Jewish Talmud. The Torah and Masoretic Text has "unseemly" and "obnoxious." What a fine predicament all this makes for us! The result, as anyone might suppose, is ambiguity and a wide division of opinion. This divided the nation in a very major way, as we shall see.

In the first century before Christ, the rabbinic schools of Shammai and Hillel were locked in controversy over the meaning of this term and the true cause for divorce. The school of Shammai interpreted nearly all the biblical laws strictly and rigorously. They held that only sexual immorality was cause for divorce, a view completely at variance with the customary right of the husband in Israel. The school of Hillel, on the other hand, was generally more liberal, holding that the husband need not assign any reason whatever for divorcing, since anything that displeased him was adequate cause. The ancient tradition seemed supported by Hillel and it eventually prevailed.

One hundred years later the question was still the subject of debate. A commanding authority, Rabbi Akiba, held with the school of Hillel, as did Philo of Alexandria, one of the most distinguished philosophers and jurists of his time. A noted historian, Flavius Josephus, also shared this view and wrote: "He who desires to be divorced from his wife for any cause whatever, and many such causes happen among men, let him in writing give assurance that he no longer wishes to live with her as his wife." And a glance at the *Encyclopedia Judaica* of our time endorses the opinion of Hillel in interpreting the phrase to mean any kind of obnoxious behavior or mannerism. How trivial indeed were the causes commonly justified by citing this Scripture! Jesus came at a time of easy divorce.

John Murray deduces that the following facts bear most cogently against the view that this passage refers to adultery:

1. The Pentateuch prescribes death for adultery (Lev. 20:10; Deut. 22:22–27).

2. Numbers 5:11–31 provides for cases of suspected adultery, but the penalty is not divorce. The charge of sexual uncleanness against a newly wedded wife is dealt with in Deuteronomy 22:13–21, but it is not by divorce.
3. The law provides for all kinds of contingencies in the matter of sexual uncleanness, but in not one of these cases does this phrase occur, and in no case is there recourse to divorce.

What are we to say? Two things impress themselves upon us. *First*, our expectation is that in matters of legal prescription and proscription the most precise, unambiguous language will be employed. Certainly we expect this in the language of Mosaic law, for God is the Author of every word of it. *Second*, the history of interpretation leaves no doubt but that the crucial phrase nevertheless is ambiguous. Even when pointedly asked what it meant, our Lord did not take the opportunity to clear up the controversy. While He left it in ambiguity, He did come down hard, adding, "And I say to you: whoever divorces his wife, except for unchastity, and marries another, commits adultery" (Matt. 19:9). In our next chapter we shall consider at length what Jesus meant.

It may come as a surprise to learn that there is no further instruction on divorce and remarriage in the entire Old Testament. But then we are reminded that there is very little instruction about marriage either. Mosaic law assumed the right of divorce, attaching little importance to the formalities or consequences. As to cause, the law seems deliberately ambiguous. Never was it a matter for the Jewish courts to decide. There were no civil or ecclesiastical penalties, nor was there any custom of social ostracism. Divorced and remarried persons were not put out of the congregation, nor was their covenant participation jeopardized in any way. There were no pronouncements of God acting as constraints. The procedure itself was as simple as it could be. The husband wrote out a bill of divorce on his own behalf, keeping to the prescribed words, and returned his wife's dowry. The bill read (as later examples show) like this: "Let this be from me your writ of divorce and letter of dismissal and deed of liberation, that you may marry whatsoever man you will." So what we have in the Old Testament is a gracious concession, arising out of God's provisional will for a people whose sin and failure brought about the breakup of marriage. *It was a provision of grace.*

When we turn to the New Testament, the question naturally arises as to whether there will be a more rigorous law of divorce and remarriage under the New Covenant. How will our Lord take His stand with reference to the Mosaic permission? In what way will His kingdom ethic transform Mosaic law into something higher? After all, we do not live under Mosaic provisions. But as in every other matter of spiritual concern, the Old Testament is preparatory to the New, and what we learn of the nature of God and His provisional will can only serve to illumine our New Testament study. It is the New Testament from which we take our cues.

Remarkable Demonstration of God's Grace

There is an extraordinary illustration with which we close this chapter. Of the highest significance, it roots in the Old Testament, but its consequences do not appear until we come to the New Testament—and to nothing less than the very genealogy of Jesus Himself.

Our attention is drawn to David and Bathsheba. David, you recall, sinned grievously when he left his armies in the field, returned to the palace to indulge himself in leisure, and there in idleness was faced with strong temptation. His eyes fell upon Bathsheba as she bathed, and his lustful heart induced him to commit adultery with her. To cover his sin of adultery he plotted the death of her husband, Uriah, one of his closest friends and a great general of the army. Much later, when Nathan was sent of God to confront David with his sin, David fell into great remorse and repented of his sin (see how his penitent heart overflows in the words of Psalm 51). God forgave David and purposed to bless him mightily, although David was allowed to suffer the consequences of his sin in his family life. In our emphasis upon forgiving grace, we must keep in balance the complementing truth: *sin is never without consequences.*

David had already taken Bathsheba to be his wife before he was brought to repentance—a very poor beginning indeed! Yet God allowed that marriage to stand. All the more amazing, God blessed that marriage begun in adultery, all because the past was forgiven. Matthew's Gospel takes special care to indicate that the Messiah's line came through David by Bathsheba, or "by the wife of Uriah," (Matt. 1:6). What a bitter reminder of David's sin and God's incredible grace!

Now, if the adultery of David and Bathsheba was forgiven by God and the marriage blessed and put in the very genealogy of Jesus, then, in Jay Adams's question, "Why do we say that persons who are forgiven and cleansed before marrying (*or*, we would add, *remarrying*) cannot expect God to bless their marriage because of sin in their past?" Who are we to restrict God's forgiving, renewing grace?

So it is that our examination of the Old Testament reveals God's provision for divorce and remarriage and, although set in the context of Mosaic law, we have glimpses of God's gracious ways.

5

Jesus and the Pharisees

Our attention now turns directly to the New Testament, first to the words of Jesus in the Gospels. In the four places where Jesus is recorded as speaking to this subject—all four in the first three, or synoptic, Gospels—two have special significance, and both are in the Gospel of Matthew.

The first is in Matthew 5, which contains the first part of the Sermon on the Mount, a very special context that calls for a separate chapter later on. In terms of what Jesus teaches about divorce and remarriage, Matthew 5 adds nothing specific. It is the context in which He speaks that calls for special consideration.

We are reminded immediately that our only claim to understanding the mind of Jesus, in whatever text, is that we first set His words in their proper context. The context always places limitations upon what is taught, whether the narrowest of applications or the widest possible. Sometimes what Jesus says is limited to answers given to specific questions. If, then, we generalize beyond these contexts, we invite false teaching. Serious exception is to be taken to scholars who ignore or violate the contextual limits of a given passage of Scripture. Too often, I fear, this is done in order to make the scriptural teaching fit their own bias or presuppositions. In other words, Scripture is made to teach what they want it to teach. But responsible teachers must discipline themselves to first understand their own presuppositions and biases, then be as careful as possible not to allow these to govern their method of analyzing Scripture or the conclusions and applications drawn from it. In this study I have sought to be aware of my own bias and presuppositions. The reader is invited to watch for this.

It's All in Matthew 19

Our attention focuses on Matthew 19:3–12, a passage often regarded as the highest development of Jesus' sayings on the subject of divorce and remarriage. It contains the greatest number of components to be found in any of the accounts. It is the most pivotal of the four, distinctive in that it alone contains the combination of two clauses, *the exceptive clause* and *the remarriage clause*. Each of these appear elsewhere (in Mark and Luke), but only here are they coordinated. But before we turn to the detail, we are well advised to note that Jesus is speaking within a particular context. The adage has it that "a text out of context is a pretext"—usually for asserting one's own opinion or bolstering one's own presuppositions. It is especially critical to the understanding of Matthew 19:3–12 that Jesus' words not be stripped of their historical, cultural, or contextual setting. And perhaps it is well to declare from the start that our method will not be simply to collect texts or cite declarations. Any ethical issue must be regarded within the larger ethical framework of the New Testament. As we shall see, this is a framework of "realized forgiveness"—James Emerson's fine term—and of ever-renewing grace.

The passage begins by setting the scene—so all-important. It is a debate scene: "And Pharisees came up to him and tested him by asking, 'Is it lawful to divorce one's wife for any cause?'" (v. 3).

Notice the obvious limits of this situation: Jesus is faced by Pharisees, Jewish religious authorities, who came for one purpose only—*to test Him*. It is not as though Jesus gathered His disciples and said, "Now I'm going to teach you

everything the church will need to know about divorce and
remarriage—how it is now under Mosaic law, how it will be
in the coming messianic kingdom of perfect righteousness,
and how it will be under the church age of grace, that interim prior to My establishing the kingdom on earth." No,
Jesus is not concerned with teaching all that, nor were the
disciples prepared to understand such complex truths. Certainly the Pharisees were not! Nor would Jesus have any
reason to attempt this at that time. While *we* need to understand what lies beyond the limits of this specific context,
they did not.

Our next consideration is of the nature of the test itself.
"Is it lawful to divorce one's wife for any cause?" First, what
did they mean by "lawful?" One thing only: "What does the
law of Moses allow?" The whole issue is limited to this point
of reference. We must not dissociate this passage from the
category of instances where Jesus and the Jewish authorities disputed points of Jewish law. When the Pharisees challenge Jesus (four instances in Matthew alone), it is always
as to His relation to Mosaic law, whether it concerned His
teaching or His conduct. The demand upon Jesus is equally
clear: He is bound to only one consideration: He must answer in strict accordance with their question, giving neither
less than they ask or more. As Guy Duty puts it, "The Pharisees had Jesus answer to *their* question, as presented by
them—and as understood by them." This is quite a different
question from what Christians are asking today! *Jesus did
not attempt to address such questions as we would ask today,
all of them outside His situation at that time.*

Interestingly enough, when a bit later on Jesus was ques-
tioned further by His disciples (vv. 10–12), He did not go into
the matter in any extended way; He stayed strictly within
the context of the question posed by the Pharisees—what
was lawful under Mosaic legislation. To assume more than
this is to court a faulty interpretation, or a risky one at best.

Clearly the scene is an attempt to discredit Jesus before
the law and at the same time involve Him in a burning controversy of the day. In the evil motivation of His detractors,

whatever side Jesus takes, He will lose out with one rabbinic school and its adherents.

Elsewhere we have described the two rabbinic schools that flourished in the century before Jesus came, the schools of Shammai and Hillel. Shammai held that only sexual immorality was valid cause for divorce, whereas Hillel included the broadest spectrum of causes. And now the Pharisees sense that if Jesus sides with Hillel, He will show Himself to be a traitor to the law as many interpreted it. But if He sides with Shammai, He will lose His popularity with the majority. They fully expect to trap Jesus on the horns of this dilemma. Our Lord's mastery of every situation is nowhere more evident than on this occasion:

> He answered, "Have you not read that he who made them from the beginning made them male and female, and said, 'For this reason a man shall leave his father and mother and be joined to his wife, and the two shall become one flesh'? So they are no longer two but one flesh. What therefore God has joined together, let not man put asunder (Matt. 19:4–6).

Jesus surprises His questioners by pointing away from the law of Moses to the orders of creation and, in so doing, does not directly answer their question. He points back to the divine institution of marriage, to what God purposed for mankind from the beginning, what He intends for all time. Yet at the same time Jesus—Himself the Author of Mosaic law, including its regulative aspects and concessions—tacitly acknowledges the right of divorce and remarriage under that law. He simply says that it was not the case "from the beginning." The original intent of God was that marriage remain indissoluble. Since that purpose has not changed, He calls them back to the fact that married couples are intrinsically one; their unity is established in God's "one flesh" purpose. So everything in their life together is to be controlled by this union; it is unique, exclusive, total, and sacred.

What God Has Joined Together

Jesus, having quoted Genesis 2 concerning the intrinsic union of husband and wife, adds His own summation and then goes on to state a fundamental principle governing all marriage: "So they are no longer two but one flesh. What therefore God has joined together, let not man put asunder."

Over the years we have all heard these words at countless wedding ceremonies. Since this is part of tradition, we quite naturally assume that the principle is binding upon every marriage, regardless of what major impediments may stand in the way of successful fulfillment. Consequently, we have entertained no questions as to whether these words might be taken in a somewhat different sense. In pastors' marriage seminars I have sometimes asked, "Precisely what did Jesus have in mind by these words?" Invariably the reply is: "God makes husbands and wives one flesh; therefore they are never to divorce." Never, under no conditions whatever? To these brethren, Jesus meant this as an absolute law, embracing all married couples without exception. So when I have gone on to ask whether Jesus might possibly have meant anything other than this, the response generally is "No," apparently it is as simple and straightforward as that. But is it? While the principle is directly intended for every couple, does this statement preclude all possibility of exceptions? This requires careful examination.

Take the case of a couple in deep marital trouble. By any biblical standard, their marriage could hardly be called Christian. It never has been. The husband resists all attempts at building a biblically informed marriage, although the wife desires this. "Unfaithful" in every sense of a covenant of unity, he will not hear of divorce. He has it too good. Ironically, he quotes Jesus to a wife he has cruelly neglected, exploited, and intimidated: "You're a Christian. You know Jesus says that what God has joined together, you are not to put asunder." He thoughtlessly believes all weddings conducted in a church are "what God has joined together." He holds this over her head.

The wife, disabled in her attempt at maintaining a Christian home and probably with biblical justification for divorce, still desires more than anything else to be faithful to Jesus' every command. So she resigns herself to the apparent truth of her husband's claim. Perhaps her pastor reinforces this decision when he, too, quotes, "What God has joined together, let not man put asunder." The declaration of Jesus has locked her in forever. With no possible exceptions allowable, she has no choice but to resign herself.

But are the words of Jesus being properly applied in such instances as this? Was Jesus speaking in binding terms to every conceivable marriage, however alienated and non-Christian its character? A closer look at the wording suggests a broader interpretation, which does not necessitate an application to every marriage, whatever its developing state may be.

Now, to be sure, the conventional interpretation is not something we are dismissing in any sense. It is to be fully accepted—*but only with the provision that it is understood as a generalization.* That Jesus' declaration is meant to speak directly and personally to every Christian couple is not to be denied. Here is a fundamental principle upon which every Christian marriage is to be built. But our point—and it is a critical one—is that Jesus is looking *beyond* individual marriages and the question of success or failure in particular marriages, *back* to the marriage institution, and *onward* to how that institution is threatened. Jesus addresses a fundamental principle, not particular couples.

The problem is that here we have a general statement of principle without concern for possible exceptions due to a couple's failure. In response to the Pharisees, why should Jesus take up aspects not relevant to the occasion? Why confuse one question with other questions? Furthermore, He could not possibly address all the extenuating circumstances that might make it impossible for any given couple to fulfill the principle of permanency. It was the principle He wished to drive home, and this He did by not introducing the question of possible exceptions that historically might prove inevitable. His declaration stands out powerfully as a single, uncomplicated statement of fundamental principle. Whatever provision must be made for a failing humanity, God's intent for marriage does not change.

One lesson in all this is that we must be cautious as to how far we can legitimately appeal to this declaration in situations where our concern is with a particular marriage suffering from serious impediments to its fulfillment. Then there are other considerations together with other scriptural principles to be taken into account. The task is to correlate separate principles.

In order that this interpretation might become clearer, let us look at it in finer detail. What clues do we find in the very wording? We will discover that there *are* clues.

To begin with, if Jesus intended this principle to apply in a binding way to every conceivable marriage without any further considerations, might He not have been more explicit in the wording of both clauses? In the first clause, might He not have used "whom" God has joined together, instead of "what"? Still more precisely, might He not have used "whomever"? As a general rule, whenever Jesus wished to enunciate a principle universally binding in every case without possibility of exceptions, He turned to "whoever" or "whomever." For example, right here in verse 9 Jesus says, "Whoever divorces his wife . . ."—the word *whoever* meaning "in every case." Twenty-one times in Matthew, "whoever" is on Jesus' lips. Why not here? Is not this the word we should expect? The word *whomever* would immediately establish the presumption that Jesus meant every married couple without possibility of exception. Permanency would be binding in the case of every marriage, however frightful the state of affairs. More than a statement of principle, it would be law; the declaration would be equivalent to a command.

But Jesus did not use "whomever," but rather the impersonal "what"—in itself no more definite than "the thing that" ("*the thing that* God joined together"). I confess that I for one believe that Jesus always spoke with deliberation. Since this is what He meant to say, this is what He said. The question is *Why?*

Had Jesus said "whomever," making the principle binding upon every marriage without regard to anything else, it would be inconsistent with at least one exception, unchastity, which He cites in Matthew 19:9. So we conclude that Jesus' word choice of "what" makes for an all-encompassing generalization. He intended to state a principle, not its possible exceptions. His declaration cannot be pressed further than this. He was not at all unmindful of the major impediments that can indeed preclude some marriages from fulfilling this divine principle.

Just *what* has God joined together (not *whom*)? The answer: *men and women in a permanent marriage bond*. He is referring to nothing less than the marriage institution. God instituted marriage for the welfare of the human family. He joins men and women together in the marriage institution with all it involves. It is a total bonding of two persons in a single life.

Now we are in position to ask what is meant by "let not man put asunder." This is the question raised by the wording of the second clause. A problem arises in each of the two clauses. Inasmuch as modern versions use a more contemporary English word, we will follow the New International Version's "let man not separate." Whom does Jesus mean by the word *man*? Had He said "whomever God has joined together," we might have expected it to continue "let not husbands separate." Or if Jesus were looking beyond Jewish times, when only husbands could initiate divorce, He might have broadened it to say "let neither husbands or wives separate." This most certainly would have established the presumption that under no conditions, however impossible, might any couple separate by divorce. Clearly it would say for all time: No exceptions! No conditions!

The word *man*, however, is not equivalent to "husbands," or to "husbands and/or wives." The word *man* refers to mankind in general. The comparative parallel is: *God* joins, *mankind* separates. God instituted a permanent marriage bond; mankind, therefore, is not to contravene God's institution by making divorce and remarriage an optional institution. While Jesus is speaking directly to Christian couples, He is saying much more. He is focusing upon the fundamental principle that informs God's institution of marriage.

If all this seems complicated and difficult to grasp, conceptualize it in this way: Both God and man institute social relationships to govern human life. At the very beginning, God instituted the marriage relationship. He did so with the intent that it be a permanent relationship of husband and wife, never to be dissolved for any reason whatever. But, in the course of time, sinful mankind also instituted social relationships, one being that of divorce and remarriage. In this instance, what man instituted is clearly a contradiction to what God instituted. In truth, what God has joined together, man *has* put asunder. Since God instituted marriage as a permanent relationship, man is not to reverse this by turning the permanent into the impermanent. Let not man dismantle God's institution! This is exactly what Hillel's school had done in Jesus' own day. This is what is occurring in our day as well.

How forcefully we see Jesus speaking to Israel in its day of laxness with regard to the institution of marriage. There were multiple divorce/remarriage cases then. Following Hillel, even the most trivial causes were upheld. Jesus could also foresee the same conditions prevailing in future times such as our own. What He drives home is the very essence of the marriage bond as God instituted it. This was His whole thrust, the primary object of His declaration. Other meanings we may attach, however legitimate, are secondary.

Now, it may very well be that in accordance with man's philosophies and psychologies, divorce is legitimate for every reason, as it is now established firmly in civil law. But this does not stand with God and ought not to govern His people.

The point of this extended examination is to show that Jesus simply and majestically set forth the general principle governing the institution of marriage, without considering individual cases where there might or might not be justifiable reason for a failure of fulfillment. Thus we must be careful not to argue cases of divorce and remarriage on the sole basis of this declaration.

Had Jesus said, "Whom God has joined together," the word *whom* would either mean that "all who marry" are joined together by God, or would refer to a particular classification of couples—those who qualify in some respect. First, then, do we suppose that those who marry, say, in a church with a Christian ceremony conducted by the pastor—that couples who marry under these circumstances—are those whom God has joined together? Or do we assume more broadly, since God ordained marriage as a sacred institution for the human family, that all who marry are joined together by Him? Either point of view would be difficult to sustain. Both biblical study and long years in the pastorate convince me that the clause "what God has joined together" cannot possibly be the equivalent of "everyone who is joined together in marriage." To take this position would be tantamount to making God responsible for every mistaken marriage ever contracted.

The most notable illustration I recall concerns John Milton, author of *Paradise Lost* and other literary masterpieces. Milton was not only acknowledged to be the greatest literary mind of his century but was a devout Puritan Christian who sought to honor God in his life. He was a keen student of God's Word.

John Milton grew up in virtual intellectual isolation, surrounded by bookish concerns, not social interests. Socially, he was immature. He was not interested in girls or in romantic contacts. At age thirty-four he was still unmarried. It was then that he met a frivolous, illiterate young woman exactly half his age. Her world was an utter contradiction of his own. Milton became enthralled with her—a classic case of emotional infatuation. Before he really got to know her, they married. She found she could not possibly live with him, so she left. Milton realized he had made a tragic mistake that could not be reversed, nor could the marriage be maintained. Since divorce was not an option to Puritan

Christians, he agonized over whether God would allow some form of annulment. The account of his agony of soul and biblical search was published in a long tract, which remains part of his extant works.

Not long afterward, this legal wife died. Milton was released from his impossible situation. His later years were lived with a wife who, through his time of blindness, proved a faithful and compatible wife—a blessing to God's literary servant.

Pastors who see their church young people marry—many of whom they themselves unite—could keep a journal over the years, with names, dates, and entries something like the following:

Whom adolescent immaturity has joined together . . .

Whom romantic illusion has joined together . . .

Whom haste and little preparation have joined together . . .

Whom sexual passion (with or without guilt) has joined together . . .

Whom an unplanned pregnancy has joined together . . .

Whom mutual loneliness and emotional deprivation have joined together . . .

Whom neurotic need has joined together . . .

Whom the prospect of getting away from a bad home has joined together . . .

Whom the prospect of financial security has joined together . . .

The list grows in proportion to pastoral experience. And pastors know that they themselves have been guilty of complicity in some of these marriages. So, in those cases where divorce followed (with few people surprised), it could be said that the mistake was not the divorce so much as the marriage itself. We are forced to ask, "Which is the greater tragedy in God's eyes, the ill-advised marriage or the divorce?" Certainly there are some instances for which we could surmise the former.

All through our study we are seeing that there are instances where divorce is the reasonable, if not inevitable, outcome of situations that ought never to have been. For yet other reasons, divorce is justifiable and remarriage the better way. But how does this square with the fact that Jesus allowed but one exception—sexual unfaithfulness?

By way of anticipation, suffice it to say that we shall find reason to conclude that *divorce is not limited to this single exception.* At the moment, this is not the focus of our study. If we hold strongly to God's purpose for marriage, recognizing that exceptions are just that—exceptions—then the problem in the world around us is much larger and more serious than the question of exceptions. Man outside of Christ, doing what seems right in his own eyes, has turned God's marriage institution into his own social institution. Man has turned the *permanent* into the *impermanent.* The institution of marriage has been changed into the institution of marriage-divorce-remarriage. Man has put asunder what God joined together.

Today divorces are encouraged for reasons not justifiable in God's sight at all. Christians, too, are caught up in this culture of the times. Too often Christians think that whatever the civil law allows is right for Christians. Even Christian counselors are found among those who counsel divorce whenever marital difficulties seem unresolvable according to their diagnosis. In such cases it is the counselors, not the couples themselves, who become the final decision-makers. Is there not a real danger in this?

Are we not to see in Jesus' declaration a warning to pastors and counselors who too-readily counsel divorce, who all but make the decision for the couples? Such decisions must be made responsibly by couples themselves, without the direction of third parties. It is too easy for couples to justify their divorcing because a counselor encouraged them to do so, thus shifting responsibility from themselves to the counselor. In the final analysis, each couple is responsible to God and to His counsel alone. Each must hear and heed God's voice as he speaks to their condition from His unique perspective. He may be preparing to do what seems utterly unlikely to either the couple or their counselor. None of us knows the mind of God or His power on behalf of troubled couples, nor can any of us give final guidance based on our perception of personalities, backgrounds, or circumstances. At best a counselor can bring some light to bear and seek to point out the consequences of whatever action the couples choose to take. What we may safely assume is that God will make His perfect will known directly to any couple who earnestly seeks Him. For this reason I do not counsel divorce. There were times in the past when I did so, much to my regret as I reflect upon it now. This decision is up to couples themselves; they must make the choice. *Let not man separate them.*

Returning to our point of departure, let it be reiterated that although we find broader perspectives and greater implications in Jesus' declaration, the conventional interpretation is to be sustained, yet only with the provision that it be recognized for what it is primarily—a generalization, a fundamental principle to govern the marriage institution. But make no mistake—every Christian couple is subject to this divine principle. To put it directly: *What God has joined together* (in your case: *you, your marriage, by your assent*), *let not man separate* (in your case: *the two of you*). This fundamental principle is to govern your marriage and is never to be abrogated (although that is sometimes permissible under general principle) save for the most exceptional, God-directed reasons.

Why the Mosaic Concession?

Not having been given an answer to their question, the Pharisees then ask Jesus, "Why then did Moses command one to give a certificate of divorce, and to put her away?" and Jesus replies, "For your hardness of heart Moses allowed [not "commanded"] you to divorce your wives, but from the beginning it was not so" (vv. 7–8). Jesus now joins the issue squarely and declares Himself. Worth noticing, too, is a reversal of terms. In Matthew, the Pharisees' question was couched in the words, "Why then did Moses *command* . . . ?" In His reply, Jesus was careful to say "allowed" instead of "commanded." This is reversed in Mark 10:4–5, where the Pharisees said "allowed" and Jesus speaks of a "commandment." Is there a reason for this? Yes. In Matthew Jesus is concerned with the bill of divorce, whereas in Mark He recognizes divorce as a social reality that required regulation. The important observation here is that in Matthew Jesus is careful not to let it seem that divorce was commanded by Moses, only permitted as a concession to human failing.

Jesus' phrase "for your hardness of heart" is an Old Testament expression that the Pharisees understood. It stood for any sinful resistance to God's direction (for a New Testament usage see Ephesians 4:17–18). In the present connection it may mean that marital conflict—with its anger and frustration, its hopeless despair and inability to reconcile—further breeds a stubborn, unyielding unwillingness to try to make the marriage work. In my marriage classes I reminded my students that marriage is made in heaven, but God gives it to us in kit form! It works only if we make it.

A marriage partner can harden himself or herself against the demands of the marriage ideal until it is too late and the damage is irreparable. This is an ever-threatening condition. In a Christian relationship, marital disappointment and difficulty can be exacerbated because the unfulfilled ideal was so high to begin with. Or should one person want a Christian marriage and the other not respond, the desire of the one may put the other under deep conviction and subsequent unhappiness. Yet, if there continues to be unwillingness, the result can be a truly hardened heart. This is one route to an ultimate collapse of marriage.

In the Beginning

Now what did Jesus mean by "but from the beginning it was not so" (v. 8)? A principle developing in this study concerns different administrations of God's will in different periods. During man's innocence, when perfect righteousness characterized his relationship with God, he was governed by God's absolute, unconditional will. There was but one will in the world—God's will. There was but one righteousness—God's righteousness. After man's fall, different conditions came into existence, which called forth a different administration of God's will. His relationship with fallen man incorporates no change in purpose and intent, only change in the manner in which His purposes shall now be administered. God's governance of man becomes provisional for the first time. *God accommodates to man's inability to live in perfect righteousnessness.* There is now mercy and forgiveness; this is the new dimension of God's governance, not necessary at "the beginning." His grace is larger than man's sin, more dominant than His own judgment. Sadly we must confess it—*sin has changed mankind radically, and this calls for a radical adjustment in God's moral governance.* It is in this sense that Jesus said that "it was not so" in the beginning. Farther back than any debatable causes for divorce is God's original purpose for marriage, designed for an environment free from sin and disobedience to the covenanted unity of two spouses. There was no need for any provision for divorce and remarriage. Therefore, before the Pharisees can begin to understand what God was then permitting by way of divorce and remarriage, they must see His initial intent—what marriage is meant to be, what God's standard is. Against this, all discussion of divorce must take place. *Thus Jesus' primary objective was to reaffirm God's purpose and standard for marriage.*

We must be careful to note that Jesus did not go as far as many of His interpreters. He did not say, "As it was in the beginning, so it must be *from now on* for all who follow Me." No, Jesus was not suggesting that we can go back and recreate the pristine conditions that prevailed at the beginning, the kind of world in which there was no fallenness, where only perfect righteousness ruled. Nor can we conclude that Jesus was denying the place of divorce in the fallen world, the world of which His people are an integral part. He was not proposing a restoration of the world of perfect right-eousness as a present possibility. That will come true in the future kingdom, over which He in His glory will reign. What we have in Jesus pointing to an ethical context vastly different from the one which He and the Pharisees were dealing. Tacitly, this is an acknowledgment that contexts do change in God's administration of His will, and that the ad-ministration of His will changes accordingly. That His gov-ernance is provisional we know, but in exactly what ways we shall pursue throughout this study. *Our problem is to know the nature of the ethical context in which we live as the church, and how God administers His will for us.*

The Heart of the Matter

We come now to the crucial declaration of Jesus in answer to the Pharisees, "And I say to you: whoever divorces his wife, except for unchastity, and marries another, commits adultery" (v. 9). Clearly, Greek scholarship understands "ex-cept for" to signify an exclusion—*an exceptive cause for which an action is rightly taken.* Divorce and remarriage are unjustifiable in relation to God's perfect purpose except for "unchastity" (the English word used in the Revised Stan-dard Version and the New American Standard Bible). The King James Version used "fornication," found also in *The Living Bible.* The New International Version has "mari-tal unfaithfulness."

The Greek word is *porneia.* It is complex and inclusive. But the primary thrust of the word is sexual immorality in general, or sexual immorality of specific kinds. The presti-gious study of *porneia* in the *Theological Dictionary of the New Testament* lays special emphasis upon "adultery" as the primary connotation. Now, "fornication" is the most common meaning of the term, connoting unlawful sexual intercourse, and this may apply to a variety of sexual acts. When fornication is committed within marital relation-ships, that is, with a person who is not one's spouse, then it is rightly called "adultery." So, while there is a distinct Greek word for adultery *(moicheia)*, the word *porneia* was used in order to refer specifically to adultery within the marriage and yet remain inclusive enough to refer to other forbidden sex acts that might be present to break the constitutional bond of marriage. Thus *porneia* was used in the Septuagint, the Greek translation of the Old Testament, to refer at times to incest, sodomy, bestiality, and other forbidden sex acts (see Lev. 20:11–21).

Evald Lövestam is a recent scholar cited by William Heth and Gordon Wenham as enumerating rabbinic texts where the Hebrew *zanah* refers to a wife's sexual unchastity, leading Lövestam to conclude: "Against this background the most plausible interpretation is without doubt that *porneia* in the exceptive phrases in Mt. 5:32 and 19:9 means sexual unfaithfulness. If the intended meaning was any other the term used would have been highly open to misunderstanding."

With reference to forbidden sex acts covered by *porneia*, it can be said that while adultery was condemned by the Jews, Greeks, and Romans alike, polygamy was approved by the Pharisees, making this a problem in Jewish life. While condemning polygamy, Romans allowed for concubines as well as a wife. Technically, both polygamy and concubinage are tantamount to adultery against a wife. This is added cause for Jesus to use the word *porneia* to cover the range of unchaste acts that intrinsically break the sexually constituting bond of marriage.

In a more distant and obscure sense, *porneia* referred to invalid marriages, but only because such marriages involved the illegitimate use of sex. Strangely, some prominent Bible teachers in our day are teaching that the exceptive clause of Jesus in Matthew actually does not refer to adultery at all, but only to illegitimate marriages in the time of Jesus, and hence the exception has nothing to do with marriage in our time. This is an entirely false direction to take, and the reader will note that Appendix B is devoted to the refutation of this notion. It is not a widely accepted interpretation, for very good reason.

Curiously, Jesus entered the debate, not to take sides with

either rabbinical school, Shammai's or Hillel's, but only to give His own judgment. His perspective supersedes the law of Moses and all its interpreters. He alone is Judge.

The exceptive clause teaches that beyond the question of the Mosaic law, and more in keeping with "the beginning," *divorce and remarriage are permissible only for adultery against a spouse.* Only adultery is intrinsically justifiable as a *cause* for divorce-remarriage, since it violates God's purpose for sexually exclusive bonds in marriage. Adultery breaks the constitutive bond that sex represents, and in fact it accomplishes a real dissolution of that bond. Two things then can happen at this juncture. Either there is forgiveness and a restoration of the exclusivity of the sexual bond, or there is divorce. Divorce, like marriage, involves consent, and when one partner initiates the divorce against the other's wishes, consent is only partially present. It is on the principle of mutual consent in all things marital that we say that the person not giving consent becomes the "victim" of divorce. While the bond between husband and wife may in fact be dissolved by adultery, divorce is not actual until there is willful action to make a legal dissolution. One partner or both take responsibility.

That Jesus allowed but one intrinsic cause for divorce in His confrontation with the Pharisees is not enough to conclude that adultery is the only cause for divorce ever. What it does teach is that *all other causes are not intrinsically justifiable,* although any one of them constitutes sin against God's covenant purpose. Just precisely what is meant by "adultery" must be taken up in detail later. However, it is not too early to indicate the author's position, viz., *that cause for divorce may not be the central issue in the biblical ethic,* even as it is not the big issue of our time except in a diminishing circle of believers. This is not to say that adultery as cause for divorce is reduced in importance. We must never forget that Jesus singled this out as the one cause that intrinsically breaks the marital bond. We read in Ephesians 5:3–6 that fornication is not even to be named among the saints, that fornicators have no inheritance in the Kingdom of Christ, and that because of fornication the wrath of God comes upon the sons of disobedience. It is thus perfectly understandable that fornication and all forms of unchastity are an utter abomination to God and constitute the moral cause that more than all others destroys the sacred marriage bond and leads to divorce.

If the notion that adultery is not the only permissible cause for divorce—if indeed it is possible (if not probable) that the basic notion of "infidelity" to the covenant of marriage includes much more than physical infidelity—if this thinking at first seems new and bewildering at this point in our study, may I suggest the reader hold all response until adequate attention can be accorded this theme in later chapters. Here I shall do little more than suggest this line of thinking.

What Breaks the Covenant of Marriage?

Along with sexual intercourse as constitutive of marriage, there must be *consent* and *commitment*. And if marriage is truly marriage as God intended, there must be a loving, caring mutuality. This being true, the death of marriage may very well be from internal causes, not external such as adultery. When consent and commitment are retracted for whatever reason—in all likelihood because love is lost and there remains no emotional bond—marriage may continue to maintain itself as a sexual relationship but be "marriage" in name only. Spouses may continue to live together in the convenient arrangements of a common home, but it is a marriage in name only. We can argue, with mature understanding, that sexual union is constitutive of marriage if, and only if, it presupposes a union of heart and mind, spouses committed to each other in all the conditions and obligations of married life. Sexual acts, as intimate as they are, hardly constitute marriage where a common life and union of mind and heart are absent. It is the intimate life and love of two people that lead to their natural expression in sexual union, not the converse. The physical acts of marriage, in other words, are not marriage itself. Yes, marriage implies sexual acts and is incomplete without these, but it is not merely a contract for such acts. Marriage is a personal commitment leading to a total way of life, a shared partnership at all levels of being and doing. *Marriage is more than a sexual relationship, and unfaithfulness is more than adultery.*

The question remains as to why Jesus made unchastity— violating the physical bond of marriage—the single violation for which divorce is validated. All through Scripture the theme of sexual exclusivity in marriage is mandated. This is the constitutive bond because it is symbolic of the total union of persons in mind, body, and spirit. So intimate is sexual union when it is fused together with love and commitment that it is the unique carrier of emotional and spiritual meanings. The biblical perspective is that marriage incorporates sex; sex is designed for marriage; and both sex and marriage need to be fused in the bonds of love. God appoints sexual union within marriage as the sign and symbol of intimate and loving personal union. There is no more fundamental violation of the marriage union than violation of the sexual bond.

Now we are in position to go back to something Jesus said early in His response to the Pharisees. He said, "Have you not read . . . 'For this reason a man shall leave his father and his mother and be joined to his wife, and the two shall become one flesh.'? So they are no longer two but one flesh. What therefore God has joined together, let not man put asunder" (vv. 4–6). The first thing Jesus says to the Pharisees is descriptive of the nature of the marital bond, indicating what they knew to be most centrally constitutive of that bond.

When we read "one flesh," we are prone to jump to the conclusion that this refers exclusively to sexual union. But this is far too narrow; the term is more inclusive than that. In the Hebrew, the word *flesh* has a variety of possible meanings, depending upon the context in which it is used. Some meanings are simple and straightforward, such as "skin." Others are more comprehensive, standing, say, for "mankind" ("all flesh"). The clue to its meaning in this passage comes from a curious fact: *the Hebrew language has no word for personality, for the totality of personal being.* No word, that is, until we discover that it employs "flesh" for this concept of the total person—personhood. The word came to mean "one's whole embodied self." Thus the phrase "the two shall become one flesh" stands for this: *two persons, a man and a woman, each his or her total embodied self, truly joined together in a union of spirit, mind, and body.* This, then, is marriage, the biblical meaning of "one flesh"—two persons in their totality, bonded in a total relationship.

It remains inescapable that Scripture places large emphasis upon the significance of the sexual bond. It is the bond exclusive to the two spouses, thus especially constitutive of their union. The depth and mystery it represents is symbolic of total personal union. As we shall see later, *it is symbolic of the depth and mystery of the union between Christ and His church.*

Otto Piper wrote that the biblical view of sex revolves around the sanctification of marriage as the God-given goal of sexual relationship. When sexual union forms one dimension of a bond that includes love and commitment, we begin to grasp the magnitude of the meaning of marriage. The highest form of human commitment, marriage, unites the most intense pleasure, sex, and the highest emotion, love.

Modest reflection is sufficient to see why marriage and sex are integrated as they are. Marriage is the properly ordained context for the fulfillment of God's purpose for sex. Marriage purifies and stabilizes sex, making it a responsible act rather than a casual or exploitative act with no deeper meaning for true relationship. Marriage gives sex an appropriate role in representing all that marriage is as a covenant of unity and fidelity.

Since sexual bonding is also the means of procreation—children being the living extension of a united pair—a further significance attaches to its role in marital bonding.

Inasmuch as children brought forth from sexual union represent the life of both partners, children further the symbolism of marital oneness.

It becomes increasingly evident that when this sexually constitutive bond is broken, violated by adultery, it then is symbolic of the breakdown of the whole marital union—a breaking of the covenant bond itself. Adultery is destructive of all that stands for unity between two persons. Furthermore, from that adultery may come illegitimate offspring. Thus we have multiple reasons for understanding why God sees adultery as intrinsic cause for divorce. The legal severance gives recognition to the broken bond at the very heart of a covenant relationship. Thus the essential reality of marriage hinges in a fundamental way upon the exclusivity of the sexual bond.

Let us be quick to point out that the grace of a forgiving spouse can in some instances be the means toward marriage restoration. For this we can be profoundly grateful. The Book of Hosea is God's picture of such forgiveness and restoration, also showing this to be God's first priority when marriage breaks down. He is glorified whenever such restoration takes place. Still in all, the destructive nature of adultery and its consequences are plain to see, and they are often so utterly devastating that God's permission to divorce for this cause is perfectly understandable. Whatever else men and women find as justifiable cause for divorce, Jesus goes only so far in His dispute with the Pharisees as to declare that there is one intrinsically justifiable cause. He focuses upon the bond of unity and fidelity most profoundly symbolized by the sexual union. In the light of this, *what intrinsically breaks that bond is sexual infidelity.* For His debate with the Pharisees, this answer was entirely adequate.

Silence of Mark and Luke

A careful student of Scripture may be puzzled if not disturbed by the fact that the clause of exception—"except for unchastity"—is not found in Mark's or Luke's account of this saying, whereas it is found twice in Matthew's. Many solutions have been advanced that are not persuasive to this author. Most of them attempt to reason why a choice must be made between the absolute prohibition in Mark and Luke, and the qualified prohibition in Matthew, which makes an exception for sexual unchastity. The trend seems to be in favor of rejecting the exception clause in Matthew as having been added by him and thus not the actual saying of Jesus. Several reasons are proposed as to why Matthew might have made this addition on his own so as to speak more acceptably to his particular community. The present author finds this suggestion totally unacceptable.

Think for a moment—you who believe God to be the Author of Scripture—would Matthew, a chosen recorder of Jesus' teaching, be so bold as to intrude an exception of his own making where Jesus had made none whatever? Would he deliberately counter an absolute prohibition of Jesus expressed here or elsewhere? Or would he be ignorant of the fact that the other Gospel writers heard the statement as an absolute prohibition? Or would the Holy Spirit, who divinely superintended the work of each Gospel writer, allow this radical reversal to be represented as that of Jesus if it were not?

No, it need not be a matter of choosing the statement of one Gospel writer over another, and certainly not a matter of explaining why Matthew might have added something Jesus did not say and could not have meant!

In proposing a solution to this problem, it is necessary to provide a bit of background information concerning the special contexts in which Mark and Luke wrote. Here we find a satisfactory clue for their omission.

We assume that Mark's full account (Mark 10:1–12) is parallel to Matthew's, that these are of the same identical event. In each Gospel the episode follows the note that Jesus went to the region of Judea. Each records how the Pharisees came to test Jesus. Immediately following the account, both Matthew and Mark go on to tell about bringing the children to Jesus. This in turn is succeeded by the account of the young man who came asking Jesus how he might inherit eternal life. The sequence in both Gospels is identical. Furthermore, there is no reason to think these to be different instances, other than that certain elements of the story differ. But here the requirement is one of rather simple harmonization.

What arrests our attention is that in Mark the story is shortened. The crucial statement of Jesus is not found at all in His words to the Pharisees, as in Matthew. But it *is* found in Jesus' private conversation with the disciples. We can assume from the two accounts that Jesus made the declaration twice, but differently to the two groups. Is it a contradiction, or a matter of what Jesus wishes to teach each group? We believe it to be the latter. This is the clue to harmonization.

The response of Jesus to the Pharisees demanded some word as to what causes for divorce were legitimate according to His interpretation of Mosaic law. So Jesus, having informed them that marriage, at its very heart, is a bonding of husband and wife in a unique unity of persons, proceeds to teach them that sexual unfaithfulness breaks that intrinsic unity as profoundly as anything can and hence is a justifiable cause for divorce in God's sight. The unity is in fact broken, destroyed.

The occasion of His responding to the Pharisees did not call for anything more, certainly not an extended discussion as to what a theology of marriage would incorporate when God's people were no longer under Mosaic provisions. When men and women under New Testament revelation would understand a deeper personal bond, there might well be a comparable understanding of how that bond could either be violated or in one sense or another repudiated. So Jesus' reply to the Pharisees can only be said to have been complete enough to have satisfied their question within the context of Mosaic law. And it was exactly that!

Mark is notable for a shift in context as it relates to this saying of Jesus. After Jesus finishes with the Pharisees, He converses privately with His disciples, who wanted to know more. No longer having to deal with the question of cause for divorce, Jesus now makes His declaration to the disciples in terms of the absolute, creative intent of God. He speaks of the unconditional will of God, that foundation upon which marriage is to be built so as to meet God's ideal. It is a permanent union that provides for no dissolution for any cause whatever. In the purpose of God, there are no exceptions. Jesus does not go into what may occur when specific couples fail to meet the ideal of marriage as a bond of unity and fidelity. He is driving home the fundamental principle and nothing more—that marriage is an enduring bond, meant to be permanent through all circumstances.

Thus, you see, we can distinguish the two different purposes, which led Jesus to frame His declaration differently. Each is sufficient for the group of persons He was addressing. We see no problem in the two accounts. There is no contradiction, no insoluble problem.

The Perfect Standard

To the student of the New Testament Epistles, the most significant thing is that Jesus is concerned at this point to harmonize His teaching *neither* with Mosaic provisions on one hand, *nor* with redemptive provisions of the New Covenant on the other. As to the question of forgiveness for failure, or of renewal by God's grace to new beginnings, nothing of this even enters into the narrative. Here Jesus is concerned *only* with teaching the truth of God's perfect righteousness with reference to marriage, only with what is God's unconditional will for His people. He does not concern Himself at this juncture with such matters as the application of His provisional will for redeemed people who are still wrestling with human weakness and failure. In fact, it is not in the synoptic Gospels at all that realized forgiveness and renewing grace are developed theologically, but in the Epistles in their ethical instructions to the church.

Does the Exception Apply to Both Divorce and Remarriage?

Some scholars hold that the exception clause only applies to divorce, not to remarriage. It is this author's opinion that *both* divorce and remarriage are comprehended under the exception, an opinion reinforced not so much by Greek syntax as by contextual and theological considerations. Admittedly, had Jesus meant the exception to apply *only* to divorce, the Greek construction would be the same as it is. Admittedly, to make the exception apply to *both* divorce and remarriage clauses, it *might* have seemed better construction to have the exception come after the second clause "and marries another." Our contention is that there is more involved in understanding what Jesus had in mind than Greek syntax. There are three weighty considerations.

First, Jesus is talking about divorce and remarriage *together,* not divorce alone or remarriage alone. Therefore, in the exception clause, coordination of divorce and remarriage is naturally assumed, unless a superior reason indicates otherwise. If Jesus did indeed intend to include remarriage in the exception, the dual application we find in His declaration—so concisely put—drives home Jesus' point. This is what we should expect, inasmuch as the Pharisees did not question the right of remarriage after divorce, their assumption resting solidly upon Old Testament grounds. Jesus fully intended to show that perfect righteousness in demonstration of God's design for marriage required the recognition of a sinful element whenever remarriage followed divorce, except in cases of unchastity.

Second, remove the exception clause and what do we have? The sentence then reads, "Whoever divorces his wife, and marries another, commits adultery." Here is a general statement that coordinates the twin actions—"divorces . . . marries another." But to this coordination of actions is added an exception clause. The natural understanding is that the exception applies to both.

Since the Pharisees' test-question had to do only with the

cause(s) of divorce, how surprised they must have been when Jesus declared in one compact statement that *neither* divorce *nor* remarriage after divorce is acceptable within God's design, save when the marital bond is broken intrinsically by the sin of unchastity.

Now, if Jesus had meant to exclude remarriage from the exception, would He not have made that perfectly plain? He could just as easily have said, "Whoever divorces his wife, except for unchastity, commits adultery. And whoever remarries following divorce, *for whatever reason,* commits adultery." That the Pharisees' question had to do only with the cause(s) of divorce did not serve to limit Jesus' response to that one aspect alone. Indeed, He shows the real issue to be the coordination of divorce and remarriage and also what does and what does not make this twin action sinful. The exception indeed applies logically to both divorce and remarriage. The subject is comprehensive of both.

Third, Jesus, surprisingly enough, nowhere says that remarriage may not follow divorce. What He does say is that remarriage following divorce for most reasons contains an element of sinfulness. But He does not go beyond this. His words cannot be taken as equivalent to a prohibition of remarriage—even though the church has traditionally assumed this to be the case. We can examine the issue by means of a question: What is included in the nature of divorce as understood in Matthew 19:9? Note, we are not concerned with *causes* of divorce, but only with the *nature* of divorce.

First of all, observe that Jesus did not challenge the Pharisees' understanding of the nature of divorce and remarriage. We might expect Him to, but He did not. Since the Pharisees' question had to do with Deuteronomy 24:1–4, in compliance with that passage they were talking about *divorce with the right of remarriage.* This is how *they* understood the nature of divorce and remarriage. But did Jesus understand the nature of divorce and remarriage as they did? Or did He propose a change? We do not find Him explicitly proposing a change, nor even hinting at it.

The Pharisees used a common term for divorce—"putting away" *(apolein)*, the same term Jesus used. So we credit the Pharisees and Jesus with an equivalence of terminology. The likelihood then follows that Jesus held to the same concept as to the nature of divorce and remarriage as they. Under the regulatory law of Deuteronomy 24:1–4, it became mandatory for a bill of divorce to include the words, "You are free to marry again." Jesus nowhere so much as hinted at a change, nor did he provide any reasons why there should be. Rather, Jesus confined Himself to declaring that remarriage following divorce—for any reason other than unchastity—contained an element of sinfulness. It is this sinful element we must come to terms with, not remarriage itself. Thus we have no reason to believe that the nature of divorce and remarriage changed under Jesus' teaching; but to that understanding He added the clear note of sinfulness as an element in any divorce and remarriage outside the exception.

As we examine the teachings of Paul, this will become increasingly clear, noting especially how his counsel was qualified by special circumstances relating to the Corinthian church during a time he referred to as "the present distress."

It is most interesting that Jesus did not declare Shammai's strict interpretation to be the correct one, although this seems to have been His own position. His teaching was identical to that of Shammai in its main focus; adultery was indeed the intrinsic cause for divorce. But Jesus' use of *porneia* instead of *moicheia* makes it clear that the exception includes a greater range of covenant-breaking sin than adulterous fornication. It includes every form of invalid marriage according to Mosaic legislation, all such marriages involving in turn invalid sexual behavior. But Jesus, in superseding the Mosaic provisions, shows Himself taking His place as the One "greater than Moses" who has come to announce the higher ethic of His kingdom.

Whoever Divorces
Commits Adultery

"Adultery" has been the ominous word that throws apprehension and despair into the hearts of those who face what seems to be an inevitable divorce, or who have already passed that point. So we must get to the very heart of things and ask what Jesus meant in saying that "whoever divorces his wife, except for unchastity, and marries another, commits adultery" (Matt. 19:9) and the additional saying, ". . . and whoever marries a divorced woman commits adultery" (Matt. 5:32).

Most certainly Jesus does not mean actual adultery, for divorce and remarriage—except in certain instances—does not necessarily involve sex with someone other than one's spouse. And what one does *after* divorce is not against the former spouse and can no longer be an act of unfaithfulness. But in remarriage one takes a new sexual partner along with the remarriage. Under these circumstances, what kind of adultery has Jesus in mind?

With Ray Anderson, Fuller Theological Seminary professor, we would say, "Adultery in this sense is not the definition of one's moral life, but the definition of one's ethical relationship to the absoluteness of the marriage vow. When a party to a previous marriage relationship is still living, the remarriage always involves ethical adultery." Dr. Anderson uses the term *ethical adultery* in contrast to actual adultery, reminding us of Jesus' words in the Sermon on the Mount, "But I say to you that every one who looks at a woman lustfully has already committed adultery with her in his heart" (Matt. 5:28). This is not actual adultery but adultery fantasized, yet Jesus says it has the same moral quality and should go by the same name. It is ethical adultery—unfaithfulness to God's ethical intent. Plainly a contradiction of God's absolute ethic, remarriage carries the ethical quality of adultery. Such a judgment is naturally appropriate inasmuch as God's purpose suffers a breach, however justifiable that breach might seem in our world, where marriage dissolution is sometimes inescapable. *We must distinguish ethical adultery from actual adultery.*

When the living symbols of one-flesh union cease to exist, when love and unity of spirit are no longer present, then dissolution may become the tragic moral choice—a choice of what is perceived the lesser of two evils, hence the only positive good.

To retain marriage merely to preserve the legal bond, an image of unity that is nonexistent, may well destroy one or both persons through indignity, unreality, or bondage. As we shall see later on, this is the problem with legal separation as a solution to a couple's inability to live together. Separation solves nothing, yet perpetuates a pretense that continually eats away at reality. It is saying that something still exists, when by any measure of reality it exists no longer.

It appears from Matthew 19:3–9 that Jesus instituted two provisions that superseded Mosaic law: *He abrogated the Mosaic penalty for adultery, which was death, and legitimized divorce for this cause instead.* Jesus exercises original legislative authority as the messianic King. He is not setting down a law of prohibition for any and all divorce and remarriage. Rather, He is setting forth the perfect righteousness, which in turn puts the character of divorce in stark contrast. What is missing here is some concrete situation to which Jesus can point to demonstrate how He would actually deal with men and women caught up in marital breakup.

Inasmuch as we are presently dealing with the exception of adultery, two further matters are of importance in this connection. It has been argued that Jesus, in saying that remarriage for any other cause than adultery is tantamount to commiting adultery, must be implying that remarried persons are living in sin. But the word must be taken as a "gnomic present" in the Greek, say our experts. Since this means that continuance is not in view at all, it is not legitimate to appeal to the Greek present-indicative tense to assert continuance. Besides, we have seen that this is ethical adultery, not actual; the act of remarriage is a breach of God's purpose, hence tantamount to ethical adultery. *It is not the sexual experience of the remarrieds, but just the fact of their remarriage, that is termed "adultery."* This is one more reason why we insist that this is forgivable sin, and once forgiven, it is put behind the parties now remarried. *Remarriage is not continuing in sin.*

What About the Guilty Party?

A second matter of importance, directly related to the discussion above, has to do with the guilty party in divorce. Assuming that the innocent party in divorce where adultery has occurred can remarry, what about the guilty party? Do we impose some form of church discipline upon this person, perhaps even exclusion? Do we forbid remarriage altogether? Do we suggest that any remarriage must take place outside the church? Are we saying that ministers may not participate in such remarriage services because sin can definitely be proven?

Professor James Bales makes an acute point. When a person puts away a spouse because of adultery, the marriage bond is broken by divorce and the innocent party is permitted to remarry, according to Jesus. Since He did not address the question of remarriage for the guilty party, we do not have His mind on this. But we are not entitled to make a negative judgment based on His silence or upon our own disapproval. The answer to the question is inherent in the nature of marriage and divorce. Let us follow this reasoning.

Why is the innocent party permitted to remarry? Because innocent of the sin that broke the marriage? Intuitively we agree that this is the case. But we have a problem with even the innocent remarrying, for in Matthew 5:32 Jesus says, "Whoever marries a divorced woman commits adultery." If an innocent woman's former husband has remarried, how can her own remarriage cause another to have committed adultery? Remarriage is not sin against the former spouse; thus there is but one way to understand the term—*it is ethical adultery*. Remarriage involves a second sexual partner, whereas God's purpose was that there be no more than one, so long as that one is still alive. In view of God's purpose, it is only by His grace that even the innocent have the right to remarry.

But is there another reason why the innocent party is free to remarry? "Yes," says Bales. The former bond of marriage no longer exists; both parties are free from it, for divorce broke that bond. But observe, says Dr. Bales, if the innocent party is no longer married to the guilty and thus free to marry again, so also the guilty is no longer married to the innocent and is thus free to marry again. *The freedom is not based altogether on innocence or guilt but upon the unmarried state.* The argument seems reasonable enough. But it is the moral issue that disturbs us with reference to the guilty party. How is that resolved? There is often enough a great difference between the innocent and the guilty!

The problem has its resolution after this manner: There is a requirement the guilty must meet that is much more than what the innocent must meet: *The guilty must come to God and acknowledge his (or her) sin, sincerely confessing that he is the guilty one.* Forgiveness is received gratefully and humbly in a deeply penitent spirit. There must also be a resolve to live henceforth with renewed heart and life. Once forgiven, the sin is put away in God's sight, never again to be recalled against that one's account. It is as though it had never occurred. Now, putting away this sin in God's grace-provision is no different from putting away any other sin—great or small, more or less grievous, more or less hurtful to the other person. *Sin is sin, and forgiveness is forgiveness.*

While Jesus tightened up the cause of divorce and remarriage to one intrinsically justifiable circumstance, He did not indicate any change in the nature of divorce and remarriage from the Old Testament provision, this being perfectly understood by the Pharisees. Any change would have obligated Jesus to make it plain, and this He did not do. Jesus did not legislate the matter at all. He certainly did not even hint that the guilty party was to remain unmarried, while the innocent was not. The point is simply that what God puts behind Him in forgiving grace we must put behind us in the church. Since Jesus refused to legislate a prohibition for the guilty party, neither must we. Our one legitimate concern is that the guilty understand their sin, have a deep and true repentance, and evidence a changed life. For this reason the church is well advised to recommend that such persons delay remarriage for a substantial period of personal and spiritual renewal.

Significantly, in the Epistles there are lists of sins, carefully categorized. Adultery is one of them. But nowhere are the divorced and remarried listed as fitting some category of sin. Does this not reaffirm the view that even the guilty party to divorce, if sincerely penitent, stands within the forgiving grace of God? To the truly penitent, both forgiveness and renewal are freely available. It is as forgiven persons that all who are divorced, however guilty or not guilty, must seek the plan of God as to whether it is proper for them to remain single or marry again.

Here we face a further complication, one that affects church governance. It especially has to do with discipline within the body of Christ. Not always is it possible to know just who the guilty party is. There are degrees of guilt. The questions facing governing boards are these: Must degrees of guilt be determined in every case of marital dissolution? Does the New Testament indicate that church discipline is required? If so, what discipline might that be?

The first thing we observe is that church discipline is not required by any New Testament text. If marital breakup is accompanied by some flagrant sin such as adultery, this must be dealt with. The adulterer must face church discipline. But where there is no clearly determined guilty party, is it the business of the church to undertake a collective judgment as to the degrees of guilt to be assigned each party? If so, how might this be done? By what criteria? It is impossible to ascertain all the elements that enter into a judgment of this kind, especially the internal factors. The testimony of the parties themselves most certainly will be weighted with personal bias. Interrogation places the parties in an adversary position that may not be called for at all. Or one, possibly both, may not wish to disclose and thus make public certain facts that to their conscience may seem inappropriate. They may simply be unable to make such disclosures that are threatening to them. Defensiveness understandably tends to warp testimony. The end result can only be uncertainty at best, error at worst. And we may even wonder if a truly adequate examination could be devised. Since countless matters are not verifiable, they are of questionable value. An attempted tribunal often accomplishes little more than deeper hurt for the parties involved.

The silence of Scripture, the absence of criteria for equitable judgment, and the desire to deal justly and compassionately seem to indicate that *it is not the church's concern to judge degrees of guilt in marital breakup.* God is the true Judge. So far as the church is concerned, certainly where free and full forgiveness in God's grace is its guiding principle, the only relevant guilt is that which the divorced themselves deem appropriate to confess as a sincere token of penitence. This is the perspective we would suggest for a grace-oriented church board.

Does God Penalize Failure?

A respected New Testament scholar, R.V.G. Tasker, perceptively comments that in these words addressed to the Pharisees, Jesus is not laying down a fixed rule that must be followed by His disciples at all times in the future. It is strange, he says, that Christians—ready enough to see that Jesus is not legislating in other matters of conduct—have been reluctant to bring the same consideration to their interpretation of His teaching on marriage and divorce. Tasker adds, "No fixed rules therefore about divorce could possibly have been given which were equally capable of being applied to Christians in the first and in the twentieth centuries." Tasker supports this by showing that the only static factors are, first, that the divine ideal for the relationship of men and women remains the same, and second, that men and women remain the same frail creatures who often find it extremely difficult to achieve in a particular marriage relationship the unity that alone could be truthfully described as "a joining together by God." Tasker takes the position of compassionate permission, pointing to the story of Jesus and the woman taken in adultery found in John 8:3–11. It is helpful to review this episode.

You recall that the woman taken in adultery was accused by two witnesses, as required by Mosaic law. Jesus tacitly acknowledged the correctness of the accusation and its sentence when He indicated that they should proceed to execute the sentence by stoning her. Then He added a condition that her accusers could not fulfill: "Let him who is without sin among you be the first to throw a stone at her" (v. 7). This was Jesus' first step in preparing the way for the woman to be released from her accusers and made subject to the forgiving grace He would proffer her. Jesus Himself was the only person present who could fulfill that requirement! When the accusers slinked away, leaving the woman alone with Jesus the Righteous Judge, He said, "Neither do I condemn you; go, and do not sin again" (v. 11). He overturned the case and set her free—not free because He disregarded the law or her rightful condemnation under the law. No, He set her free on the basis of forgiving grace. Shall we then show *less* grace and forgiveness than our Lord?

If God Gifts You

The full episode in Matthew 19 has an O. Henry twist at the end—an unexpected application. We move directly to this all-important sequel for Christians:

> The disciples said to him, "If such is the case of a man with his wife, it is not expedient to marry." But he said to them, "Not all men can receive this saying, but only those to whom it is given. For there are eunuchs who have been so

from birth, and there are eunuchs who have been made eunuchs by men, and there are eunuchs who have made themselves eunuchs for the sake of the kingdom of heaven. He who is able to receive this, let him receive it (Matt. 19:10–12).

Here Jesus is speaking to His disciples in private immediately following His words to the Pharisees. The disciples respond in despair; the demand is a radical one in their eyes. To this Jesus first responds with a general statement and then closes with a personal challenge.

Jesus employs the illustration of the eunuchs to create a parallel that will illumine His teaching. Those who choose to become eunuchs do so in order to preclude marriage once and for all. They do this in order to be free for special service to God. Similarly, says Jesus, some will be called to forgo remarriage after divorce for the sake of service for God's kingdom. To those for whom this call comes, those who respond, God will give grace to fulfill this discipline. But to whom does this apply—to *all* Christ's followers, in contrast to those who do not follow Christ? Or does it apply within the circle of Christ's people, a special call to some, not all?

The anti-divorce school of thought teaches that the radical demand for no divorce and no remarriage except for the cause of unchastity is meant for all disciples of Jesus. They are the ones who can receive and act upon this demand. All must obey.

In support of this view, Jesus' words in Matthew 13:11 are cited as a parallel: "To you it has been given to know the secrets of the kingdom of heaven, but to them it has not been given." The disciples will know the secrets contained in Jesus' parables; the truth is to all Christ's followers.

But this is only an apparent parallel. In the eunuch passage it is not a matter of pitting the disciples over against non-disciples. Strictly speaking, it is not a matter of some knowing, others not knowing. The word *choreo* points beyond mere "knowing" to the capacity to obey, to act upon one's knowing. Among the disciples who know Jesus' teaching on the divorce-and-remarriage subject, some will be able to act upon it, others not.

The problem was one the disciples voiced, not the Pharisees. It is the disciples' problem. Would they be able to obey? It follows logically that Jesus is responding to those who had the problem. He is saying, "If you can receive this, receive it."

We cannot regard this as a general call to discipleship. We assume far too much if we make this a universal condition for all Christ's followers. This is not another occasion where Jesus is addressing a crowd and saying, "Let him who has ears hear." No, He is addressing disciples with a condition that may very well apply to some who follow Him. The same disciplines do not apply to all disciples, any more than all disciples are called to the same commitment of service. But this will apply to some.

If we seek a scriptural parallel, the more probable and impressive one is the thematic parallel in 1 Corinthians 7, where some are called to singlehood for the sake of devoted service to God. Here some are called to make a personal sacrifice of marriage, others not. In verse 7 Paul says, ". . . But each has his own special gift from God, one of one kind and one of another." The clear implication is that not everyone can live up to this demand, for not everyone is given that special gift. J. B. Phillips's transliteration of Matthew 19:11 captures this conceptually, "It is not everyone who can live up to this," replied Jesus, "only those who have a special gift."

In the debate passage in Matthew 19, Jesus had spoken of the inherent sinfulness of breaching God's covenant of marriage, but He had not gone on to say that this was tantamount to a general prohibition of all remarriage. Now He intimates that there will indeed be those who are called to refrain from such remarriage, but this will become an actuality to those who are able. This excludes a class of persons. For some, this call will be God's highest and best for them. For the rest, remarriage may be God's best, a positive good, all things considered. I like Colin Brown's observation and believe it correct, "Jesus' last word on the subject is formulated, not as a statement, but as a challenge." Not that it is an inclusive challenge to all who follow Christ, but a special challenge to those who can receive and act upon it in response to a special, personal call.

We conclude our examination of Jesus' teaching with the seasoned words of two major commentators: First, R.V.G. Tasker: "It is difficult, then, to feel that this section of Matthew's Gospel gives us any ground for supposing that Jesus expected His Church to become an 'anti-divorce society,' which would make no provision for 'the hardness of men's hearts' or would debar from communion those, often more sinned against than sinning, whose marriages have been dissolved."

Our concluding word comes from William Barclay, "What Jesus laid down was a principle and not a law. To fail to remember that, and to turn this saying of Jesus into a law, is gravely to misunderstand it. . . . We cannot therefore settle the question of divorce simply by quoting the words of Jesus. That would be to be guilty of legalism; we must take the words of Jesus as a principle which we will apply to the individual cases as we meet them. . . . The situation should be dealt with *not* with a rigid legalism, but with an understanding love."

Having looked extensively at the response of Jesus to the Pharisees who sought to test Him in relation to Mosaic law, we turn next to the single major passage on the subject in the Epistles. Once again we shall note how teaching is within a specific context. What Paul has to say there may or may not be God's final word to us in the situations we face late in the twentieth century of the age of grace. Let us examine the possibilities.

6

Paul and the Corinthians

It is curious that the only major reference to divorce and remarriage found anywhere in the Epistles is the seventh chapter of First Corinthians. Yes, I know, some will point to the seventh chapter of Romans. But this is not teaching on the subject, as I will demonstrate in Appendix A at the end of the book.

It is curious that First Corinthians should stand as the solitary teaching passage on our subject, inasmuch as one would suppose that such a pervasive problem in human life, certainly in our times, would surely merit fuller instruction. We cannot doubt that the Author of Scripture foresaw the history of the church into the present troubled age, when so many conditions combine to make marriage a difficult and sometimes impossible relationship. The absence of extended teaching is further complicated by the fact that Paul did not set out to teach systematically on the subject, did not take up various matters that could form a theology of marriage or an ethic of divorce and remarriage. What we have is limited to his answers to some specific questions raised by the Corinthians, questions relating to specific problems faced in the congregation. Since we are not informed as to these particular problems and do not even have the questions, we can only surmise what they were from his answers.

This, of course, poses problems for us to know just what limits we are to place upon the truths contained in Paul's answers.

Paul was not addressing *our* questions, but *theirs*. Nor could he address problems of our day, which are infinitely more complex than those of his day. The cultural background is vastly different to begin with. So when we ask, "Is Paul's word to the Corinthians God's complete and final word to us on the subject?" the answer, not improbably, is "No." We have only to read what Paul said about singleness and marriage in this chapter to be convinced that he spoke to very special circumstances. To take the liberty of generalizing from his comments would be to distort the teaching we find elsewhere in the New Testament. The ethic of any particular situation like that in Corinth must be correlated with other ethical contexts in the New Testament lest we misread it for ourselves. The local situation must be taken into consideration.

Another caution confronts us in this passage. Of all the New Testament Epistles, First Corinthians is the one most fully devoted to correcting abuses. But whenever a teacher is writing to answer a specific set of questions and to correct a specific abuse, it is not generally thought that this in any sense is a complete presentation of a theme. Nor would Paul have occasion to attempt a larger set of considerations than would be appropriate to answering what they asked. For these reasons, the chapter cannot be made to cover all marital problems and their solutions as they relate to the issue of divorce and remarriage. We will next pursue this a bit further.

To All Christians at All Times?

This interpretive question is crucial to our understanding the chapter before us. It is a very special context indeed. We do not have to look very far in order to answer the question "Should we universalize Paul's words to suit *all* Christians in *all* periods and in *all* circumstances?" Take Paul's admonitions to women as an illustration. What are the historical and cultural clues that assist us in knowing whether or not to universalize? Paul teaches that women are to keep silent in the churches, to learn truth by asking their husbands (1 Cor. 14:34–35). Does this apply to women today? Are they not to study Scripture for themselves, not to read Christian books, not to discuss Christian truth among themselves? Are their husbands the only source of spiritual knowledge?

In the first century, there were ample reasons for these restrictions. Outside aristocratic circles, women were socially and educationally unemancipated. Their place was tightly restricted in a patriarchal society. They had no status. Furthermore, they were totally unprepared to assume places of leadership or to cope with such freedom as the Gospel implied. To take certain liberties would have threatened good order and made the church a scandal in the eyes of nonbelievers, who were suspicious as it was of alleged nonconformity among Christians. All things considered, in those circumstances at that point in history, this was sound advice. But does it apply to today?

Or take the question of the unmarried and widows in the chapter we are studying. Paul admonished them to remain single as he was (1 Cor. 7:8). Are we to universalize this in our teaching today? For twelve years I taught the Christian Marriage course at Westmont College. This verse would hardly have been chosen as a theme for the course! Nor would I have selected verse 27b: "Are you free from a wife? Do not seek marriage." My enrollment would have quickly dissipated! And surely I would hesitate to have taken verse 29: ". . . let those who have wives live as though they had none." Taken out of historical context, these verses would not have made sense. Proof-texting leads to heresy!

To labor the point a bit further, Paul argues in verses 32–34 that married people are anxious about worldly affairs, while single people are anxious about the things of the Lord. Undoubtedly Paul had reason to perceive this correctly in his time and as it was relevant to the Corinthians

in their circumstances. But is this a good argument for today? Is this the reality *we* experience? Modern studies indicate that single people today in America have greater
anxiety for their place in the world and are far less stable
than marrieds, by nearly every index of indicators. In the
church the complaint is often heard that singles cannot be
counted on for long-term support. They are free to come and
go, are often on the move in our mobile society, are socially
involved to a greater degree outside the church, and do not
take responsibility with the same depth of concern as settled marrieds and their families. Social conditions are
simply far different now from those in Paul's time.

In verse 35 Paul says, "I say this for your own benefit. . . ."
Whose benefit? The Corinthians.' Is it equally for *our* benefit? This is debatable, as we have seen. Then does our view
compromise the message of Scripture? Of course not! It
simply disciplines our study, making sure we understand
what teaching aspects are to be universalized as the rule for
all times, and what are not.

Paul's final word is: "I say this . . . to promote good order
and to secure your undivided devotion to the Lord." Again,
most certainly this was wise counsel for the Corinthians at
that time. But singleness in our day is not necessarily a
stronger basis upon which to build devotion to the Lord. In
fact, the singles' quest for a mate and social acceptance, for
identity and success in early employment, for travel and
"seeing the world" while they are not tied down—all these
factors militate against undivided devotion to the Lord and
His church. The married have passed the point of being primarily driven by these particular needs and are often far
freer to settle into patterns of devotion to the Lord and His
church. *What we must conclude is that there simply is no contemporary pattern whereby we can consistently say that
singleness is preferable.*

We shall see shortly why Paul's admonitions in this chapter have to do so largely with special conditions. The foregoing remarks are intended to prepare us for this major interpretive consideration, Richard Longenecker's "circum-
stantial explanation."

Chapter 7 opens with words found no less than six times in this Epistle: "Now concerning the matters about which you wrote. . . ." The Corinthians had written the apostle Paul to seek his advice with reference to the state of affairs in their church. One such subject was marriage and divorce as it arose from the nature of several problems. Evidently, from their questioning Paul, there was diversity of opinion in the church. From what we know of the existing cultural mix, probably some of Jewish origin thought marriage obligatory, while others thought it undesirable. Paul responds by holding to the biblical roots of marriage as normal and desirable, while at the same time pointing out that in their present circumstances there was reason to regard marriage as not expedient. So he begins by saying, "It is well for a man not to touch a woman," and here the words *it is well* mean "expedient." "But" Paul continues, "because of the temptation to immorality, each man should have his own wife and each woman her own husband" (vv. 1–2). The phrase *not to touch a woman,* as Gordon Fee demonstrates, is a figurative expression for sexual intercourse. The New International version mistranslates this "It is good for a man not to marry." Paul is not advocating non-marriage as being superior to marriage. He concedes the acceptability of not marrying, but from what follows, Paul had other reasons in mind. This we shall see to be the whole point of his remarks.

In verse 8 Paul says, "To the unmarried and the widows I say that it is well for them to remain single as I do." Once more his emphasis is upon what is expedient, not mandatory or superior. His emphasis runs counter to our tendency to read this as saying that to remain single is best of all. On balance, Paul simply affirms that singleness is acceptable. His only qualification is that should the single person find himself or herself unable to live with sexual passions, *then* it is better for that one to marry. Surely, somewhere in the New Testament it is appropriate to outline the advantages to those not marrying, lest from other Scriptures we assume that for all persons in all circumstances marriage is mandatory, or almost. Such has never been the case in the history of the church. Some in every generation are called to singleness. We do not deprecate this state, although persuaded that God generally calls men and women to the larger benefits of married life and family.

Abnormal Counsel for Abnormal Times

To remain single was simply good advice for that particular time and for those particular Corinthian Christians. Just why this is the case is not left to doubt, inasmuch as Paul returns to the subject of singleness in verses 25 and following. There he undergirds his advice with reasons he had not given previously. In verse 26 he says, "I think that in view of the present distress it is well for a person to remain as he is." (Another version reads "in view of the impending distress.") Paul's counsel is conditioned by what he calls "the present [impending] distress." *Times and conditions were not normal; the advice one would normally give is not appropriate for now.* Paul, who affirms the high view of marriage in such passages as Ephesians 5:21–33, is not dropping to a lower view here. Rather, he is speaking to a particular time and situation. It would be difficult to overemphasize this!

What was "the present distress," and why did it have such influence upon Paul's counsel to the Corinthians? To understand this is first to deal with a problem of interpretation. As Leon Morris writes, "Paul's references to Christ's return are not associated with a present distress." With William Barclay and others he is persuaded that Paul was not conditioning his teaching on the possible soon-return of Christ or the difficulties of the tribulation! This would tend against the stability of the marriage institution for at least these past two thousand years. Many would agree with G. Campbell Morgan's comment, "I think he was referring to local conditions . . . to the pressure of circumstances in the midst of which the church was living at Corinth . . . thinking of Corinth principally." It is most naturally taken as indicating that Paul's friends at Corinth were at that time in unusually difficult circumstances. But does history support this? F. F. Bruce remarks that the movement that Paul inaugurated was attended by tumult and disorder wherever it spread, both in the Roman provinces and in Rome itself. On two occasions, at Philippi and Ephesus, the Book of Acts records the attack of Gentiles on Christian missionaries. On both occasions the reason was a real or imagined threat to vested property interests. Great persecution followed the great fire of A.D. 64, for which the Christians were blamed. But the persecution, launched by Nero, was a personal crime of his in search of scapegoats. Nonetheless, the era of peace was broken; the official policy changed. Twenty years later, in the time of Domitian, Christianity was recognized as a new force that by its very nature seemed likely to imperil the state. It was forthwith persecuted.

But the distress came not only from the Romans; the Jews sought to destroy the Christian community wherever they could. By this time there were Jewish centers everywhere in Asia Minor. Conditions in Palestine in the middle years of the first century were marked by years of crisis, and large numbers of people, including Christians, were already leaving the country. The Jews who refused the gospel for themselves were aggravated when their Gentile neighbors embraced it, even more so when fellow Jews became Christians.

Paul by this time was no stranger to persecution himself. Read the accounts of his beatings, of his being left for dead at the hands of the Jewish communities of Asia Minor. Corinth at that time was vulnerable. Perhaps even the destruction of Jerusalem and the possibility that this would unleash new waves of Jewish violence against the Christians were within Paul's purview.

The Greek words literally say: "the distress standing near," and can be translated as "present" or "impending" distress. This depends upon the context. Most likely, Paul was thinking of the present troubles facing the church at Corinth, but possibly also of the troubles to come. Corinth was the commercial capital of Greece, and Canon Farrar

tells of the "mass of Jews" in residence, one of the largest
colonies of Hellenistic Jews to be found anywhere. In every
part of the empire the hostility of Hellenistic Jews was
feared. Although the Proconsul Gallio had only recently dis-
missed charges against Paul (see Acts 18:12–17), the situation was explosive. Paul's advice to the local Christian
community at Corinth was full of solicitude and expediency
because of these uneasy times. He might have feared the
Christians would be under severe pressures to forswear
Christ in order to save their wives and children from brutal
torture and death. Paul would save his friends from any distress possible, from any undue sorrow he could. These were
anything but normal times, and the situation called for anything but normal counsel. Can we regard it then as counsel
for *all* times?

Can we not see Paul, contrary to his teaching elsewhere
on the benefits and desirability of marriage, saying in effect, "Considering your peculiar circumstances at present,
and the hazards you face in view of your persecutors, it is not
expedient for you to marry at this time. Remain as you are
for the present"?

Now this does not contradict the teaching that marriage
is honorable (Heb. 13:4), or that marriage is the highest
symbol of the union of Christ and His church. Marriage as a
general rule is necessary to both the full development of individuals and the well-being of society as a whole. And Paul
is careful to recognize that so far as fulfilling even his suggestion, "each has his own special gift from God" (v. 7).
As with Jesus' word to His disciples, Paul concedes that to
remain single is a gift that God gives to some, not all. But
the existence of abnormal times suggests staying single.

In verse 27a Paul says, "Are you bound to a wife? Do not
seek to be free." Here is the tacit admission that it was possible for Christian spouses to choose to be free. But Paul
says this is not fitting. He is not laying down a law of total
prohibition, but simply giving a wise, general admonition.
Nowhere does he deal with extreme situations that make
divorce a critical problem to some; he is only concerned to

tell the Corinthians that it is not appropriate to desire marital freedom and undertake easy divorce toward that end. The same conclusion can be drawn as well with reference to verse 27b: "Are you free from a wife? Do not seek marriage." We may take William Barclay's comment that Paul was convinced that he was giving advice for a purely temporary situation. If he had thought otherwise, he would never have written as he did. With this we agree.

This whole chapter is enigmatic unless one keeps in mind the background of "distress," which preoccupied Paul and governed the whole scope of his advice. It is thus not improbable at all that his advice as to divorce and remarriage was governed by exactly the same considerations. It is a matter to ponder deeply that neither Paul nor any other writer (such as Peter, James, or John) wrote about divorce and remarriage under normal circumstances. There are two possible explanations for this. Traditionally it has been assumed that the words of Jesus were decisive and final; nothing further need be said. But we saw that Jesus spoke to a specific context (we shall consider His words in the Sermon on the Mount separately). And it is of at least passing interest that nowhere in the Epistles is the saying of Jesus reiterated, a possible reason being that marriage is a relationship, which like any other is subject to failure and is to be treated as any other—redemptively—allowing the grace of God to provide a solution that moves the concerned parties into new possibilities. We are not under law but under grace. Let it be reiterated: When we fail the ethical command in one area or another, we do not face legal consequences such as penalties and prohibitions. *We face the offer of forgiveness, renewing grace, alternate possibilities.*

Specifically to the Corinthians

We turn at last to the verses crucial to our study of divorce and remarriage. Our advantage now, however, is that we should be able to view these verses in the larger context of Paul's counsel and to understand the special situation that shaped his words. We are better prepared to see his counsel adapted to those special circumstances and not apt to read into it more than that. We simply have no ground on which to universalize his counsel to include those who do not come under such abnormal circumstances as the Christians at Corinth.

> To the unmarried I give charge, not I but the Lord, that the wife should not separate from her husband (but if she does, let her remain single or else be reconciled to her husband)—and that the husband should not divorce his wife (1 Cor. 7:10–11).

First, notice that Paul is speaking to these Corinthians in all earnestness: "I give charge." Second, "not I but the Lord" indicates that Paul's counsel is based on words of the Lord Himself. To go back to Jesus' words is to find the point of agreement: *God's own people are not to divorce.* This is something that—as a basic principle—they are not to do; divorce is not God's intent. Yet, observe Paul's tone and the form of his counsel. It is not "you cannot," as though an absolute law of prohibition were being enforced. No, the principle of marriage without divorce is being affirmed as God's highest and best. Paul does not actually repeat what Jesus said. Otherwise, when he tells the husband not to divorce his wife, he would doubtless have added "except for the cause of unchastity." And why does he not? *Because Paul was only concerned with the general rule, not with problems of a special nature and their redemptive solutions.* He is content to lay down the Christian ideal as the Corinthians apparently needed to hear it. Their questions evidently had nothing to do with possible exceptions. We are driven to the conclusion that Paul did not answer questions they were not asking! And neither was he concerned at the time with questions we in the twentieth century might ask.

"To the married I give charge, not I but the Lord, that the wife should not separate from her husband . . ." (v. 10). The word *separate,* according to Arndt and Gingrich and other standard Greek lexicons, signifies "divorce," which separated in the sense that it divided the couple and dissolved the union. The Greeks did not recognize a separation that left marriage undissolved. Had Paul meant only "separation," he would necessarily have had to explain that at this time or risk being misunderstood.

The Roman Catholic Church, in its teaching of no-divorce and no-remarriage, claims 1 Corinthians 7:10ff as support, asserting that the passage allows separation only. Not only is this a misinterpretation of the Greek word, but it asks for something that often does more harm than good. Separation speaks of a situation left unresolved one way or the other. It places marriage in limbo. Legal separation is recognized today as fraught with all manner of problems and is legally untenable. *Separation may often be the greater of two evils and in no sense a positive good.* Certainly separation does not meet the requirements for fulfilling Christian marriage obligations, and certainly it does not meet the requirement here that "God has called us to peace" (v. 15). Separation may provide temporary relief, but not peace. There can be no genuine peace where a relationship is left unresolved. In this very chapter Paul admonishes couples not to separate except for short seasons and good reasons, for it opens the door to temptations (v. 5). Counselors who recommend separation of a temporary nature for couples in deep conflict have often seen their recommendation backfire, since separation on these terms has paved the way for the more permanent separation of divorce.

Attic law not only allowed the husband to divorce his wife for any cause, but the wife could also demand divorce by applying to the Archon and stating her reasons. And since divorce was very common and easily obtained in the Greek world, Paul may well have been making a strong case to counter this widespread custom. At any rate, why would he open up the subject of exceptions and complex causes if that was not called for by the Corinthians' questions? We really are left to wonder how Paul would have answered questions having to do with extreme cases.

In verse 11 we have a parenthetic clause: "But if she does, let her remain single or else be reconciled to her husband."

Here is practical recognition of the possibility that the ideal will not always be obeyed. Paul's advice is a departure from the teaching of Jesus, for Jesus did not make this recommendation. And why did Jesus not recommend reconciliation? Because He was talking about divorce on the grounds of unchastity only and was obviously not about to advise a return to an adulterous partner. Surely Jesus would not give spouses the right to divorce for the cause of adultery and then turn around to command them to be reconciled with their adulterous partner. In fact, Jesus stated a principle, but He did not follow it with any suggestions as to what actions were to be taken.

Good Advice If . . .

Think about Paul's advice for a moment. It is good advice *if. . . .* If what? *If it were possible*—that is, if the husband had not already remarried, or if she could return under circumstances that promised success. Since Paul knew the situation he was speaking to, there were no *ifs;* he knew the real possibilities in this case, and he spoke to those. We can only say, "Good advice, *if. . . .*"

Let us return to the observation that Jesus did not prescribe what action should be taken. He only addressed the principles involved in divorce and remarriage insofar as the perfect righteousness of God and His design related to the law of Moses. *We* are the ones who tend to take Jesus' declaration and presume to advise what action is or is not to be taken. Sadly, what we so often prescribe is a legalistic prohibition, which we consider right but which has no basis in Scripture.

Is it always best for a divorced woman to remain single? Was this always best even in Paul's day? Or was it best just in the Corinthians' circumstances that Paul was addressing? Singleness in Paul's world was a fearful thing for a young woman. The Jews felt marriage was obligatory. A "single" woman could return to her father's home but need not. By custom she was not to be out on her own. This would signal a runaway, a castaway, or a prostitute. She would have no means of livelihood except in servitude. It was hardly the life normally recommended!

"For it is better to marry than to be aflame with passion" (v. 9). Paul is speaking here to singles. But is this less true for divorced persons? Surely the divorced are those most seriously affected by having once known sexual fulfillment but now to be deprived in their present state. Are they not the more likely to be "aflame with passion" and vulnerable?—"It is better to marry."

Verse 11 also reads: ". . . the husband should not divorce his wife." But be reminded again that the Lord (whom Paul claimed as his authority for this word) made an exception for adultery. Does this mean that Paul is talking about divorce on grounds other than unchastity? Does he then hope for reconciliation because there is less reason for divorce, one of the easy divorce cases so prevalent in his day? *He certainly must be referring to a situation where there was some genuine ground for reconciliation.*

These are difficult questions. If nothing else, they caution us not to look for a full set of answers to today's complexity of divorce cases—not in this passage! And we can be sure of one thing, that Paul was not content merely to quote the words of Jesus and assume that they would settle everything. Paul's recommendation in the problem brought to him by the Corinthians was very restrictive, but perhaps that was the best advice he could give in view of the kind of marital problem they posed to him. As for us who have no way of knowing what the particular circumstances were, it serves as a strong word of caution. May we, too, be slow to encourage divorce, quick to find ways of reconciliation or of holding off divorce action wherever there is hope. This is the primary message to us.

There is one other consideration here. Paul's admonition to remain single may very well be in line with what he has been saying about singleness throughout this chapter—that it is to be preferred in a time of "impending distress," whether for the never-married or the divorced. Although we cannot dogmatize about this, it is a reasonable assumption. Beyond this, we may add that Paul is strongly reinforcing the ethical ideal, apparently sorely needed by the Corinthian church, one further area of Corinthian laxness that Paul must deal with in this letter. With such a basic need to experience Christian marriage and to move away from customary easy divorce, the Corinthians did not need to have Paul go into exceptions that did not apply, perhaps inviting further temptation to divorce. There is a time and place to discuss God's grace in response to marital failure, and a time *not* to discuss this among immature Christians by whom it might be misunderstood. It would be for the same reason that I would not suggest putting this book in the hands of a person contemplating divorce, lest it be construed as supporting their action. Paul may be giving us a picture of pastoral wisdom by not bringing up every facet of divorce and remarriage with the already-troubled Corinthians.

When the Spouse Is a Pagan

> To the rest I say, not the Lord, that if any brother has a wife who is an unbeliever, and she consents to live with him, he should not divorce her. If any woman has a husband who is an unbeliever, and he consents to live with her, she should not divorce him. . . . But if the unbelieving partner desires to separate, let it be so; in such a case the brother or sister is not bound. For God has called us to peace. Wife, how do you know whether you will save your husband? Husband, how do you know whether you will save your wife? Only, let every one lead the life which the Lord has assigned to him, and in which God has called him (1 Cor. 7:12–13, 15–17).

Here is a new question, a new situation for Christians in Paul's day: How should they judge the dissolution of a pagan-Christian marriage? In what ways would this differ from the dissolution of marriage between Christians?

Paul first warns the church against Christians' taking the initiative in divorce for the mere reason that the partner is a pagan. A new Christian in a bad marriage especially might think, "Well, Paul teaches us not to be unequally yoked together with unbelievers. Now that I'm a believer, I'm in that very situation. It must be all right for me to divorce him and no longer be unequally yoked."

So Paul points out that this is *not* a justifiable reason. But notice that Paul does not go into the question of a pagan husband who is also an adulterer—so common at that time. Nor does he bring in any other aggravated problem. He simply addresses the fundamental question of whether Christians should divorce pagan partners simply because they are pagans. Clearly the answer is "No."

Having laid down the general rule, the apostle proceeds to the more urgent and specific question: What if a pagan partner wants out of the marriage? This was not uncommon. When the Corinthians became Christians, they sometimes faced the dilemma of being married to a non-Christian. As pagans they had been harmoniously matched, at least in their pagan ways. But now they are not. Sometimes the believer faced violent displeasure on the part of the pagan spouse for being Christian. Sometimes this eventuated in the pagan seeking divorce. In view of Jesus' words, this was cause for anxiety. Was such a divorce valid, when the pagan partner instigated it? Should the Christian spouse try to ward it off if possible? Should one resist or cooperate?

Paul's counsel cannot possibly be squared with that of many evangelical pastors across the land. If the pagan wants a divorce, Paul says, "let it be so" (v. 15). He is saying, "Don't fight it; don't refuse it. In fact, don't call in the pastor to try to stop it. Let it be!"

Now, had Paul not believed this to be right, had not the Spirit of God directed him, he might have argued in this fashion:

> Well, really, you know you are one flesh, so marriage is indissoluble. This means you are married forever in God's sight whatever happens. Divorce is not legitimate for any

reason except adultery, so God will have no part in condoning the divorce, even if your husband is a pagan. And remember, too, that if you are divorced, you must remain single, or you will commit adultery and God can never bless you again. There will be severe consequences for you. And it is imperative that you remain single, just in case he's converted and wants to return to the marriage; you must keep the door open. Jesus didn't say anything about letting a pagan husband divorce, so surely you will fight this with everything you have. Don't give in! God will honor you and save your mate.

This has all the marks of our traditional way of handling such a possibility. But this is not Paul's counsel!

No Longer Bound—To What?

It is almost startling to hear Paul say to the Christian divorced by a pagan husband, "In such a case the brother or sister is not bound" (v. 15). Not "bound" in what way? The word carries the meaning, "to bind, to make a slave of, to hold by constraint of necessity or law." But which part of this definition applies here? We may easily eliminate what does not apply. Marriage is not "to make a slave of" (Does anyone wonder about this?), and marriage is not "to be held by constraint of necessity." This leaves two applicable meanings—Marriage "binds," and marriage means "to be held by constraint of law." The negative in this verse means "no longer bound, no longer held by constraint of law." The former contract is no longer binding. Whenever a slave was set free and declared "not bound," his former owner had no further claim upon him. The slave was given a bond of relinquishment, a contract of renunciation. This is exactly what the bill of divorce did for marriage. *It meant freedom from all that the marital bond implied.* John Murray and others who have written helpfully would agree with the summary of Geoffrey Fisher, "But clearly St. Paul's direction is that a valid marriage may in these circumstances be ended and a new marriage entered into."

There is a remarkable feature of this passage—*the believer is not obligated to try for reconciliation.* The marriage bond has been severed by divorce, and the Christian spouse is free to remarry. But the rule obtains in this case, too, that a believer is not to marry an unbeliever, even if that unbeliever was formerly one's spouse.

What is most striking about this whole passage is that Paul is not content to rest the case at this point. He has said that the Christian spouse is to let the other partner go and is free to remarry—no strings attached. But there is more. The rationale that follows is indeed striking, for it plows new ground for New Testament ethics.

Scale of Relative Values

Verse 25 continues, "For God has called us to peace." What is this but an indirect way of stating that at the heart of true marriage is peace—not unresolvable conflict, not a hopelessly divided household, not one spouse intimidating the other, not the anguish of noncommunication, not the pain of psychological abuse! No! *Where there is Christian marriage, there is peace!* And, in some pretentiously Christian marriages, we must acknowledge that peace is totally nonexistent!

Commentator F. W. Grosheide writes:

> If, therefore, circumstances are as Paul describes them, the Christian will resign himself to the divorce. If, due to the conversion of one of the spouses to Christianity, peace has disappeared in a given marriage, divorce is permissible according to the apostle. This peace is not the same as absence of domestic quarrels; it is *an internal peace granted by God* as a blessing upon a good and right marriage. If this peace would be broken by the continuation of a mixed marriage, then the yoke of bondage need not be shouldered but divorce is permissible [italics added].

I would add to this that peace undoubtedly carries a broader meaning than emotional calm. Peaceful coexistence requires a harmony of action that makes for stability of spirit and behavior. Peace of mind and action is of the very essence of Christian marriage! So is spiritual peace!

So, when peace is absent, has ceased to exist, marriage has lost an essential value. If peace cannot be reinstated, the marriage is dead. It remains only to be recognized by divorce. *Peace is the greater good, divorce the lesser evil.* For a destructive marriage, the very opposite of peace, is an evil. To retain it legally without effecting a change in the non-peaceful, destructive conditions is to mock the very nature of marriage. This, too, is a sin!

Can God relate to such a decision? Of course! His provisional will takes consideration of man's weakness, sin and failure. His provisional will centers in grace, forgiveness, and renewal.

The striking new ethical consideration that Paul introduces in this phrase, "God has called us to peace," has enormous implications. He is speaking of relative values. There is, he suggests, a higher principle than merely trying to retain a marriage contract and living together as man and wife. That higher principle is a relationship with peace. But wait! Jesus never said anything like that! He never even intimated that a marriage might better be dissolved if peace could not be maintained. Yes, I realize that Paul is applying this to the case of a pagan married to a Christian. But the essence of it is also inherent in Christian marriages, is it not? Paul is describing the very heart of a Christian marriage. He is saying that though marriage ought not to be dissolved, there are more important values than that of preserving the semblance of marriage as a formal contract or a sharing of the rituals of living together. *Divorce may follow when certain values are at stake,* in particular the value of peace, which is intrinsic to marriage. The principle that leaps out at us is this: Marriage is made for persons, not persons for marriage! Personal values are superior to institutional values, if and when one set must be chosen over the other. Persons are not to be sacrificed in order to preserve a legal figment. In an oblique way Paul is saying there is a cause that is also at the heart of marriage and divorce—the value of peace. Interestingly, in ancient Roman culture and law, this would be perfectly understood. The jurist Ulpian later reflected this and said that divorce was permissible for the sake of domestic peace.

"All Things Considered"

What must be perfectly evident to the student of New Testament ethics is that for the Christian community living within the limitations of a fallen world, there is a scale of values that involves choices. Daily we face choices that govern our ethical conduct. On the scale there are "higher" and "lower" values. The very highest value always expresses the pure will of God, His perfect righteousness. This is the goal of moral choice for the earnest Christian. But conditions are not always conducive to making the highest choice, and sometimes we must choose the highest value on an "all things considered" basis. This translates into a value that falls somewhere below the perfect ideal. Commonly this occurs whenever two sets of values are in tension.

For any one of us, scarcely a day passes but what we are confronted with decisions in which there is no perfect option. Take an example: If, in the course of driving down the street, a pedestrian steps off the curb without looking, walking right into the path of your car, a sudden choice must be made, and there is no time to think (or pray) about it. It involves the risk of hitting the pedestrian if the course is maintained (you are "in the right" to do so), or possibly hitting an oncoming car head-on if you choose to swerve in the only other direction possible. The options no longer include a risk-free choice. In fact, your choice is the one that you perceive as the lesser of two evils. That becomes the only possible positive good. You can do no better. Regardless of your high intentions, this is the kind of world you live in, and it requires your adapting to it as best possible.

The principle before us is simply this: *Where no absolute good presents itself as the preferred choice, then morally the most justifiable of remaining options should be chosen.* It is a question of "all things considered." The hope is that "a lesser evil" can somehow be transformed into "a positive good." If Scripture teaches us anything in this connection it is that God is able to transform evil into good. That He delights to do so is the record of Scripture. The greatness of God is manifested in His redemptive response to the tragic moral choices that make up history. This is true as respects every person's history.

In the case of marriage, the top value on the scale is God's creative design and purpose, namely, permanent, indissoluble marriage. Of course, there are other values that cluster around this central objective to flesh it out, as it were. These would include loving commitment to the welfare and happiness of the other, willingness to make personal sacrifices for spouse and family members, caring attitudes and actions.

Realistically, since this is not always possible to achieve, *a lesser ideal may have to be the highest value of choice "all things considered."* In the most extreme instances, this may involve what in itself is an evil—divorce. After the greatest thought and prayer, pastoral help, and perhaps professional counseling, and with a commitment to make the marriage work if at all possible, divorce may yet be the only option "all things considered." Divorce may appear to have the best promise for the future welfare of everyone concerned. The tragic moral choice is made, very possibly with agonizing doubt. There seems no other option, although it is readily acknowledged to be a tragic moral choice.

Readers may be unfamiliar with the principle being expounded, and may wonder if this is not some recent theory. On the contrary, it is a well-grounded principle of ethics. Justification of divorce and remarriage as the lesser of two evils can be traced back to the church fathers in no less a person than Origen. In the earliest centuries the Eastern church differed from the Western church in permitting remarriage after divorce.

Would Professing Christian Spouses Fit Here?

All of this is presented in 1 Corinthians 7 within the context of the Christian married to a pagan. The pagan spouse wants a divorce, and God instructs the Christian to "let it be so." But may we extend this to the marriage of professing Christians in some manner? Is there a similarity here that, although Paul did not deal with this aspect, would qualify for the same counsel? We can only speculate, but there is a moral parallel that seems quite clear.

When a Christian spouse wants out, that spouse has truly renounced the covenant of unity and fidelity, has in fact renounced God's purpose and calling. This is tantamount to an act of unfaithfulness, albeit not sexual in nature. Inasmuch as spiritual faithlessness is called *"adultery"* in the Old Testament, thoughtful scholars raise the question of whether we are not talking about a form of adultery. Would this case come within the parameters of Jesus' thinking with respect to intrinsic unfaithfulness? We cannot dogmatize, but it is not improbable and merits further scholarly examination.

Gene Getz, Jay Adams, and others have suggested that another Scripture may speak to this in principle:

[Jesus said:] "If your brother sins against you, go and tell him his fault, between you and him alone. If he listens to you, you have gained your brother. But if he does not listen, take one or two others along with you, that every word may be confirmed by the evidence of two or three witnesses. If he refuses to listen to them, tell it to the church; and if he refuses to listen even to the church, let him be to you as a Gentile and a tax collector" (Matt. 18:15–17).

The New International Version (and others) translates the last words as "treat him as you would a pagan. . . ." That is, treat him as an unbeliever. Imagine, one who is recalcitrant in this way is to be treated as an unbeliever! If this is a valid principle, we may properly ask, "If a professing Christian spouse will not respond to Christian counsel, will not listen even to the church's counsel, and will not attempt to make the marriage Christian—all the while insisting he or she wants a divorce—should not that spouse then be treated as a pagan? And, if so, would it not follow that Paul's counsel might be: "Let the married partner get a divorce; the brother or sister is not bound"? It is not an improbable application of a scriptural principle. Interestingly, Martin Luther inclined toward this view. The difficulty we have here is that we do not have scriptural examples to follow for sure. This is a judgment call.

Let's Be Realistic

Paul continues to reinforce his counsel that the Christian spouse is free to remarry by adding a practical question that is the essence of realism: "Wife, how do you know whether you will save your husband? Husband, how do you know whether you will save your wife?" (v. 16). Traditionally this has been interpreted along these lines: "Let your mate separate for a while; you are not bound to live with him or her for such a time. If you play it wisely and trust God, who knows, you may win him or her to the Lord." This is tantamount to saying, "You're not really free; you'd better not remarry or you might miss the chance to win your partner to Christ and have him or her return."

This is not what it says! Paul is advising, "Be practical and realistic. Don't place your hope in such a questionable possibility. How do you know whether you will save your spouse? You don't." This correlates with the previous sentence, "You are not bound," to indicate that the Christian is free indeed, not coerced by being pressed with a dim hope.

Now, had Paul meant to encourage the Christian spouse in this situation to go along with the divorce but remain unmarried, living in hope that the partner who divorced will come to Christ and return, he could easily have worded it to read, "How do you know but what . . . ?" This Paul did not do, and the whole previous argument shows his intent to be "You do not know whether or not; you can have no certainty." Consistency demands this interpretation to fit the chain of reasoning.

I am confident that Paul would acknowledge the noble intention behind a spouse's continuing to hope and wait for the other's salvation, keeping the door open for such a possibility. But Paul is directed of God to be realistic. *Nothing in Scripture encourages us to expect that God will always perform the miraculous.* In this matter God gives no promise, no guarantee. Although the hope for an unsaved husband's salvation is found in instructions given in 1 Peter 3, this is in a different context altogether from that of a divorced spouse, and we cannot make a direct application here.

Now, lest we be misunderstood, surely it is a wonderful thing whenever a Christian's faith and waiting is directed of God and then rewarded by Him. Like the returning prodigal, this should bring great joy to everyone. On occasion, thankfully, this does happen. But God is simply and realistically saying, "Don't claim conversion and return as an inevitable result of faithful waiting. You're not bound by an optimistic expectation or by an obligation of faith or faithfulness. You are not bound, period. You *can* remarry."

A Dramatic Declaration!

Of utmost importance to our whole scheme of interpretation is 1 Corinthians 7:27–28. It is critical that we interpret this passage within its larger context, verses 25–38. The anti-divorce school's interpretation of this entire passage is curiously varied, at the same time invariably going beyond what is *said* in seeking what is *meant*. In the process Paul's words are made unduly complicated. Yet if Paul says what he seems to say, then we do indeed have a dramatic declaration, a startling and unexpected pronouncement. In fact, it establishes the thesis of this book in a remarkable way. So we dare not gloss over these words as so many commentators do. Nor can we treat them superficially or carelessly, as many others do. Incidentally, I find my own conclusions very similar to those of Colin Brown, Professor of Theology at Fuller Theological Seminary. Others, too, are increasingly taking a deeper look at these verses.

The New American Standard Version faithfully translates the Greek of verse 27 as "Are you bound to a wife? Do not seek to be released. Are you released from a wife? Do not seek a wife."

Some anti-divorce interpreters claim that from the context of verses 25–38, it can be established that "wife" can only refer to a betrothed Jewish virgin. The assumption is that this is the proper interpretation of verses 36–38 and in turn this provides the key to verses 27–28. After all, they claim, from verse 25 right on through verse 38, the text speaks about virgins; all we need to determine is the status these virgins occupy, and this status will hold throughout. These interpreters find only one option.

Is this a correct assumption? We think not. However, the Revised Standard Version translates "betrothed" consistently in verses 36–38. The New International Version translates "the virgin he is engaged to." But it is our contention that these translations and the assumption upon which they are made are unwarranted, as closer examination will show.

A more likely alternative for the status of these virgins in verses 36–38 awaits our notice, and this in turn makes it far less likely that our key passage, verses 27–28, refers to the betrothed. And if Paul does not concern himself with betrothed Jewish virgins in *these* passages, then nowhere does he do so. The reason for this also becomes obvious with further examination.

Back to verses 36–38. The New American Standard Bible translates *parthenos* (virgin) as "virgin *daughter*", the italics indicating that *daughter* is not present in the Greek, but supplied to make sense. The word *parthenos* simply means "virgin"; there is no internal indication as to the virgin's status. Is she a betrothed virgin—in the sense of Jewish betrothal laws? Is she simply a virgin daughter—as commonly understood in Greek life and thought? We believe the latter to be the correct view.

To make *virgin* mean "betrothed virgin," whether in verses 36–38 or in our key passage, verses 27–28, an interpreter assumes that these references must somehow mean a Jewish young woman pledged in marriage according to Jewish betrothal customs; interpretation requires it in the mind of the interpreter. So let us see why the interpreter is so disposed in this direction.

Recall that in Jewish life a couple was first formally betrothed for a period generally extending up to one year before marriage was finalized and sexually consummated. Notice at once how different this is from engagement as we understand it. The couple assumed marital obligations, were called "husband" and "wife," yet during the betrothal phase of their marriage they were not permitted to cohabit or have sexual relations. If, during the betrothal period, they separated because of sexual infidelity on the part of the woman, a bill of divorce was required of the husband. It was called a divorce, as when Joseph thought to put away (divorce) Mary privately during their betrothal because of her then-as-yet-unexplained pregnancy. But how does this make room for legitimate divorce in *this* situation, but under *no other* circumstances?

Assuming that *virgins* means "betrothed Jewish maidens," anti-divorce interpreters transliterate verse 27 to read "Are you bound by betrothal agreement to a wife? Do not seek to be released from it by divorce." The verb *released* is necessarily understood to mean "divorced," inasmuch as divorce was required to end betrothal to an unfaithful woman. For this reason the New International Version actually translates it "divorced." Note what follows.

Paul's second question can then be transliterated, "Are you released [divorced] from a wife? Do not seek a wife." While nowhere is a person prohibited from seeking a wife following a betrothal divorce, Paul has consistently advised against marriage for *anyone* during this time of "the impending distress," so there is nothing unusual about this.

We have noted that this interpretation is consistent with

the anti-divorce interpretation of the exception clause in Matthew 19, for that, too, is made to apply only to betrothed Jewish virgins—a position we have rejected. To this school of thought, the divorce of the unfaithful betrothed poses no problem, inasmuch as it is not seen as having anything to do with the marriage bond as we understand it in non-Jewish culture. The key is that betrothal divorce does not dissolve a sexually established one-flesh union, for in betrothal marriage the sexual union is not yet consummated. There is no one-flesh union to dissolve! So, to these interpreters, Paul is tacitly affirming Jesus' exception relating to divorce and remarriage. Only in the case of a Jewish betrothal is divorce and remarriage permissible because of infidelity. This is denied all others whose marriages represent the one-flesh union. That union cannot be dissolved.

I have presented this position in all its logic in order to show that it all makes good sense—that is, until a few critical items are introduced. Then this interpretation becomes highly suspect. Our task is to show where the premise is incorrect.

Paul opens this extended section at verse 25 by addressing the case of virgins—not *betrothed* virgins, just unmarried virgins. There was no such class as *unattached* virgins; they were either betrothed to a husband or continued as a father's daughter. The idea of a "father's virgin" was a common one, for unmarried virgins were still under their father's authority. Greek fathers, like their Jewish counterparts, had authority over their daughters that included the right of disposal as to when and whom their daughters would marry.

It is critical to know whether the passage in verses 36–38 is speaking of betrothed daughters marrying, or simply virgin daughters who may be given in marriage by their fathers. This is settled by the verb *gamizein,* which does not occur in Greek literature prior to New Testament times but in the New Testament regularly means "to give in marriage," not "to marry." Our verses are speaking of virgin daughters who may be given in marriage by their fathers.

We follow the New American Standard Bible in this conclusion. In view of Paul's preference for singleness in those abnormal times of "impending distress," it follows that he would here suggest that it would be better for fathers not to give their daughters in marriage, but to keep them during this troubled time as their virgin daughters and continue to support them though they be of age.

Having determined that verses 36–38 do not refer to betrothed Jewish virgins, we ask next whether verses 27–28 have any greater possibility of referring to betrothed virgins, as some would like us to believe. We think not, and here's why.

What most seriously casts doubt on the betrothal interpretation is the recollection that Paul was the apostle to the Gentiles and is writing to a Gentile church, the church at Corinth. While this congregation contained some Jews, it was predominantly composed of Greeks. Paul refers to the congregation in the words, "when you were heathen" (1 Cor. 12:2). Those Greeks neither followed Jewish betrothal customs nor would be well informed about the laws governing them either. They could hardly have cared. So Paul most assuredly is not writing with Jewish betrothal cases in mind—else would he not have made this perfectly clear to the Greek congregation, which naturally would suppose that "wife" meant just that? Would we not expect Paul to have been more explicit, saying, "Are you *betrothed* to a wife?" instead of "Are you *bound* to a wife?" We can only conclude in fairness to the language and context that Paul is speaking about husbands and wives in the full sense of marriage as non-Jews understand marriage. The burden of proof certainly lies with those who hold otherwise.

With this preparation, we can consider a dramatic development in Paul's counsel, something utterly unexpected, and totally disconcerting to the anti-divorce school. In the New American Standard Bible, immediately following his two questions in tandem—"Are you bound to a wife? Do not seek to be released [divorced]. Are you released [divorced] from a wife? Do not seek a wife"—Paul adds this bombshell:

"But if you [the released, the divorced] should marry, you do not sin. . . ."

Can Paul possibly mean what he so plainly says? We must be very sure of his words, his sentence connections, the limits of the context. We must wrestle with the question of the compatibility of this declaration with Paul's advice earlier in the chapter, and also with Jesus' words. A big order, but by no means impossible.

So utterly unexpected is this statement, and so contrary to historical interpretation, that the Revised Standard Version dodges it by having the second question read, "Are you free from a wife? Do not seek marriage," making it appear to readers unfamiliar with the Greek that Paul is asking singles a question totally unrelated to his previous question and so having a far different meaning.

Curiously, the New International Version also backs off at this point, as though Paul's declaration were too unconventional to be translated straightforwardly. But having already translated *divorced* as the meaning of *released* in the first question, why not here in the second? It is the same Greek word. Or at least why not have translated it literally—*released*? The choice of *unmarried* is unwarranted.

With misleading translations appearing in some of our best versions, it is mandatory that we understand what Paul does *not* say as well as what he *does* say. We may be certain of three things he does *not* say:

First, he does not say, "Are you free from a betrothed virgin?" The word *parthenos* appears in this chapter, but not here!

Second, he does not say (as does RSV), "Are you free from a wife?"—meaning, "Are you single, hence free from a wife?"

Third, he does not say (as does NIV), "Are you unmarried?" The word *agamos* (unmarried) appears four times in this chapter (vv. 8, 11, 32, 34), but not here!

Is there a fourth possibility? Yes; we will take that up a few paragraphs from here.

Someone is sure to ask why Paul did not use a more common word for divorce if this is what he meant—like *chorizo, aphiemi,* or *apolyo*?

There are two reasons that seem compelling. First, Paul chose the word that most closely emphasized the thought he had in mind. It was a term he could use in both questions, a term that ties both questions together as interrelated. That term is *lyo* (loose, set free). One reason to choose the term *released* lies in the question itself. That question is not, please note, "Are you married?" If it were, Paul would doubtless have used a more common word to say, "Do not divorce." Instead, his question is, "Are you bound to a wife?" The word "bound" is *deo;* in apposition is the term for being released from being bound. *Precisely.*

That *released* means "divorced" is clear from the absence of an alternative. The New English Bible renders it, "Has your marriage been dissolved?" There is no other possibility.

Now, if the second question was unrelated to the first it might be interpreted variously. William Orr suggests that "Are you released from a wife?" might mean that the wife presumably had died. But since the same word *released* appeared in the first question, we need only apply this suggested meaning to see its absurdity. For then we have, "Are you bound to a wife? Do not seek release through her death." We are reminded of the anecdote of the wife who anguished over conflict with her husband. A consoling friend asked, "Have you considered divorce? to which she replied, "Heavens, no! *Murder,* yes, but *divorce* never!" No, Paul is not singling out widows; he addressed them earlier (vv. 8–9). But the consideration is far from a simple one.

Conceivably—and I find this persuasive—Paul selected the word *released* for these two interrelated questions in order to have *an inclusive term* at the point of the second question. "Are you released from a wife (whether through divorce as I've just suggested, or possibly by reason of your wife's death)? Do not seek a wife. But if you who are released in either of these ways should marry, you do not sin." This accounts perfectly for the tandem use of the word *released*. One word covers both possibilities—those previously married but now divorced, and those previously married but now widowed.

There is a clinching argument for those who still insist that the reference is to betrothed virgins who are being advised not to marry if they have undergone betrothal divorce. This argument is appropriate at this juncture because we needed first to arrive at the punch line—verse 28.

Paul wipes out the betrothed-virgin possibility by making a crucial distinction of subjects. He says (note the subject), ". . . *you* have not sinned" (NASB). This corresponds with "Are *you* bound to a wife? . . . . Are *you* released from a wife?" in verse 27 (italics added for emphasis). But watch out now! Paul switches subjects; it is no longer "you" but "a virgin." And with the change of subject comes a separate, distinct pronouncement: ". . . and if *a virgin* should marry, *she* has not sinned" (italics added). Two subjects, two pronouncements, and Paul has covered both cases—the divorced and the virgins. Case closed!

A tenacious anti-divorce advocate may still ask, "But how can you be so certain about this?" At the risk of extending the discussion beyond reasonable requirement, may I invite any persistent questioner to follow a careful bit of exegesis. Take your New Testament and read carefully from verse 24, through verse 28. Verse 24 looks like the conclusion to a discussion now closed. This conclusion repeats a principle enunciated in verse 20 to the effect that a man should remain in the condition in which he was called. But wait, does verse 24 conclude a passage? No, not really. In verse 26 Paul returns to this theme and restates the principle in a new context.

What is highly significant to note is that Paul weaves more than one theme together in these verses. It is a mistake to see but one subject; the subject changes. Although in verse 25 he begins to speak about virgins, he immediately interrupts his thought, taking up once again the theme of what is "good for a man" (NASB)—not "a virgin". He continues on this theme into the middle of verse 28. He refers first to a married man, then to a divorced man. But if he wants to talk about virgins as well, when does he do so? Not in verse 27! He returns briefly in verse 28, then at greater length from verse 32 on.

It seems very much as though verse 25 about virgins was inserted too early, inasmuch as it is interrupted and postponed so quickly. One observation provides the solution to this. Paul wants very much to include virgins as part of the general disclaimer that shocks us in verse 28. Against all his previous emphasis upon the undesirability of marriage, whether for singles, widows, or divorced persons— "undesirability" explained as his concern for their well-being during *the present* [*impending*, RSV] *distress,* Paul nevertheless wants it known that for any of these classes of persons it is not sin for them to go ahead and marry. He wants to include virgins in this pronouncement.

It is as exegetes fail to observe the switch in subject that attempts are made to relate verse 27 to virgins, especially betrothed virgins, inasmuch as marriage is involved. How totally unnecessary is all of this!

It remains to ask the big question. Is not the interpretation being proposed a direct contradiction to what Paul said so clearly in the early part of the chapter to these very same Corinthians? Did he not disallow remarriage? Does not an apparent contradiction demand some other interpretation more in harmony with that earlier passage? We will face this directly and boldly.

If it is determined for sure that remarriage of the divorced is always out of question, then this will seem radical indeed. But is it our task to conform interpretation to our presuppositions? What we need, it seems, is a creative sense that can perceive the ethics of divorce and remarriage as expanding and developing as New Testament revelation progresses. We need dare to believe that Paul is introducing a progression of ethical thought as he moves from the abnormal times of "the impending distress," and the abnormal counsel that goes with it, to what is more normative for the church at large through coming ages. What we can be sure of in this seventh chapter of 1 Corinthians is that *Paul consistently promotes the idea that marriage and remarriage are not preferable under the present circumstances as they relate to the church at Corinth.* Both marriage and remarriage will be affected adversely by the impending distress. He is fully aware that divorce and remarriage abrogate God's creative intent that there be but one spouse so long as the two are living. Human sinfulness is involved in any dissolution, however unavoidable it might be. In an ethical sense it can be called adulterous—a breach of the marriage covenant. Although—apart from the single exception, which has to do with the breaching of the one-flesh union—all divorce and remarriage involve abrogation of God's purpose, in the end this may nevertheless serve a larger purpose for good—everything considered. It may serve a long-term good, transcending the sinfulness of the present. So we can say that remarriage necessarily involves a sinful element, but remarriage in and of itself is not sin. This is in harmony with Paul's startling declaration in verse 28.

What Further Need Be Said?

Perhaps before leaving Paul's teaching, it might be mentioned that there are no further exceptions besides the one Jesus conceded—probably because this whole aspect of the subject does not enter into Paul's response to the queries of the Corinthians. It simply may not be the all-encompassing problem we tend to make it. We have seen that the very nature of the circumstances in which Jesus' exception was made force us to ask whether there may well be other considerations requiring yet other exceptions. This cannot be answered directly from Scripture anymore than many other relevant questions concerning divorce and remarriage can be answered from Scripture. At a certain point in our questions we find ourselves limited to making deductions from principles that bear directly or indirectly upon the subject. This inevitably creates some ambiguity, a factor that teachers of God's truth find difficult to cope with. Whichever side of the issue one finds himself or herself on, it is dangerous to dogmatize. What we are responsible for is to probe all likely possibilities and to think deeply enough to recognize what those possibilities might be.

The very fact that so little is taught in the New Testament, especially in the Epistles, leads us to wonder whether God's purpose is not rather to provide the broad principles instead of prescriptions and proscriptions, leaving it to personal spiritual discretion and pastoral wisdom guided by the Holy Spirit, in this way determining solutions to individual cases. One is inclined in this direction by the very complexity of modern life and the intricate web of forces militating against marriage. Paul could not have understood these mounting complexities in his day, let alone address them in a way that his readers at the time would have grasped. The twentieth century is not the first century. It may well be that today we are called upon to understand the multifaceted nature of marital breakdown, how to adequately deal with it in Christian counseling, and when to recognize the irreversible death of marriage. Take some examples that come quickly to mind. . . .

There are a variety of marriages, fraudulent or suspiciously near being so, whose nature does not become evident until some time after the wedding ceremony. One party marries, scheming to get something or avoid something, and this is not always a conscious awareness. In my counseling I have encountered the following: One party had been under psychiatric treatment for schizophrenia for a number of years. The medical contraindication for marriage was not known to the other party who entered the relationship that resulted in marriage. In fact, the psychiatric background was not disclosed for fear it might end the relationship. After the marriage the problem became apparent. The two were Christians. Either the former psychiatric patient believed God would overcome the contraindication of her doctors, or was unwilling to face the consequences. Was she deceived or deceiving? This is difficult to know. At any rate, the stress of responsibilities and intimate relationship was more than the person could cope with, and the marriage had to be terminated for the sake of both parties.

What counsel do we offer to the spouse who was victimized by this circumstance? Is remarriage prohibited for the remainder of that person's life? Or does God's understanding grace enter in to cover whatever technical sin may be involved in the divorce and remarriage?

I once had to deal with a wife who had been married some years to a man who had given her two children and a reasonably good life. Increasingly he showed strange behavior, eventually telling her that he was homosexual. He wanted a home and family, but he also wanted sexual liaisons with men, claiming that this was not adultery. His wife and children were left in a state of shock and resentment. A divorce ensued. Can this wife remarry? Is she an adulteress if she does? Pastor, what word of hope have you for her? Is your word one of prohibitive judgment or of grace and hope? Is singleness the best you can offer her?

Like many pastors, I have experienced the recounting of wives who have been terribly abused, some by professing Christian husbands who neither understood nor could account for their behavior. Sometimes it was physical abuse, at other times psychological—the abuse that takes place through unbelievable put-downs, relentless intimidation, or scorn over real or imagined faults, destroying the wife's very personhood in the process. A psychological breakdown brought this woman's situation to light. When there was no response to repeated attempts to get her husband to professional counseling, and he refused to face the necessity for change, what was left for the wife to do? She divorced.

And what of the wife married to a pathological liar, a compulsive gambler, or an addicted drinker? The home is in shambles, the children bereft of every decency, the wife dysfunctional. Again, assume that therapy has been tried without success over a more-than-reasonable period of time. What is the future for such a family? Does God's grace have a solution? Surely we can believe so!

Recently I was appraised of a situation where a family faced a shocking development. The husband was a highly respected professional in a small city and was well known for his Christian witness and leadership in the church. His wife was also noteworthy for her Christian life and witness. She had some suspicions that something was not right, but it only came to light when she caught her husband dressed in women's clothes, with makeup and all. He confessed to being a closet transvestite. Further, he planned surgery to transform him into a female—transvestitism plus transexualism. Through all this, he professed his Christian faith and devotion, insisting that this was his true nature and that he was only following the Lord's gift in making it complete. He believed he had God's blessing on his action and claimed the fault lay with people who just did not understand how God made people. What would become of his wife and family seemed strangely of less concern, for he thought that simply providing for their financial needs would be sufficient. What is the wife to do in this instance? Would you condemn her for choosing to divorce? Can she be really married to a man now changed into a woman? What is her marital status? But as a Christian can she divorce? Can she remarry? Separate only?

One thing is perfectly clear. The apostle Paul never had to deal with these kinds of situations, nor did he address them. God did not choose to make these complexities a matter for scriptural instruction. Is it not reasonable to believe that He leaves this for pastoral discretion? After forty years in the ministry, in counseling, college teaching, and pastors' conferences, I for one must believe that there is much that we cannot learn about divorce and remarriage from Scripture except by way of the principles and guidelines it provides for decision making. Scripture makes no provision for annulment, as does the canon law of the Roman Catholic Church, or we might have a mediating approach to difficult cases. The Spirit must guide us.

The question reappears: Does God stick to a legal figment, unconcerned that victimized parties suffer the cruel consequences of being unable to leave the mockery of marriage and normalize life in a new relationship? Does God wish to sacrifice all personal and family values for the sake of retaining a legal bond no longer viable? Do we have any guidance in Scripture further than the passages relating directly to the subject? I think we do. Although Jesus was under Mosaic law, He violated the law of the Sabbath in order to heal a person. When the Pharisees challenged Him concerning this violation, He justified His act by pointing to David's more flagrant violation of eating the very "bread of the Presence," a forbidden act. *In both instances, the law of necessity and the higher good of individuals prevailed over the law of prohibition* (see Matt. 12:1–8). This is Helmut Thielicke's principal point.

Not Ours to Judge

Let me reiterate that I do not personally counsel divorce, however strongly this might be indicated in a particular case. This decision must come, if it comes at all, from the parties involved. For one thing, I cannot relieve the aggrieved parties of taking responsibility for their decision. For another, I am not God; I cannot judge all the factors fully or correctly, nor can I know just when our omnipotent God may choose to change what may seem to us an impossible situation. Every counselor has witnessed the miracle-working power of God in marital chaos and marveled at the result. The task of counselors is to help individuals clarify and properly assess their situation, perhaps showing them the consequences of the actions they might choose to take— especially the potentially destructive consequences that may ensue. Of course, there are times when, despite everything, "all the king's horses and all the king's men couldn't put Humpty Dumpty together again." Nevertheless, ours should be a preventive ministry so far as that is possible.

The foregoing is the last word in the New Testament on our subject. It leaves us with a sense that a transition is taking place in the development of New Testament ethics—

from general principles and specific admonitions covering specific circumstances to a vast diversity of situations that call for pastoral wisdom, Spirit-led wisdom for individual cases. We have the sense that there are no laws covering all cases, only principles to apply as best we can with the Lord's enabling. *We must look upon difficult and complex cases as God does—provisionally and compassionately, with redemptive ends in view.* Human failing is a reality of Christian experience, even among God's choicest men and women. But God's grace is redemptive and restorative. So we adhere to the divinely ordained norm for marriage with full commitment, and we hold high the ideal. But if the ideal is missed and a failed marriage results, then we, as responsible ministers of God, must help broken and hurting individuals find the best possibilities in God's abundant provision. For some, His best may come in the form of a new marriage partner.

Remarrieds as Church Officers?

A particularly harsh prohibition in the fellowship of God's people is enforced by churches that refuse to allow divorced-remarried people to serve as church officers. This prohibition often extends further into such other areas of service as choir or teaching Sunday school. This restriction is based on Paul's words to Timothy and to Titus. A highly questionable understanding of these Scriptures underlies this discriminatory practice. Examination of language and custom gives scant credence to this view.

We are told that overseers and bishops—top offices in the church—are to be "husband of one wife" (1 Tim. 3:2; Titus 1:6). This means precisely what it says; the text cannot be translated accurately to say anything other than this. Had Paul intended to say anything else, he had exact words to do so. But the deeper question has to do with what Paul *means* by what he says. The notion that he meant "married only once," excluding the widowed-and-remarried as well as the divorced-and-remarried, has been around a long time. Curiously, it is picked up by such modern commentators as

William Barclay and given the status of legitimate translation. But the text is unequivocal and unambiguous;
it says and means "husband of one wife" (literally "a
one-woman man").

Since one looks in vain to the literature of Greek-
speaking people of that time to locate a different meaning,
an appeal cannot be made on that basis. So where, we ask,
did this idea of "married only once" originate, and especially why has it been given such prominence?

Actually this interpretation emerged in the second century as a logical consequence of the same influence of asceti-
cism that led to clerical celibacy in some branches of the
Western church. But the major ideas of the text, that which
Greek-speaking Christians would naturally understand,
was that of monogamous marriage, from the literal meaning of "one-woman man." That meaning was enhanced with
the further assumption of the husband's loyalty to that wife.
The phrase clearly meant—and most commentators today
affirm this—one wife at the time, with complete faithfulness to her throughout all circumstances. The emphasis is
upon the faithfulness and stability of the present marriage,
not upon sins or failures of the past.

What prompted this was a special problem, the common
practice of polygamy in Paul's day—a problem, incidentally,
facing missionaries in Africa today. In South America the
problem takes the form of taking a mistress, who is referred
to as one's "unofficial wife."

Paul was prohibiting the ordination of practicing polyga-
mists. Polygamy was known in first-century Judaism. From
the third century on, Roman laws bore witness to polygamy
among the Jews. Without the need for Paul to have said it in
this connection, we know that God forgives this sin as He
does every other sin, and forgiveness removes disqualification from service in the church. But one cannot *continue* in a
practice contrary to God's will. God does not forgive sin
while it is being continued. Polygamy then being practiced was a disqualification. This is Paul's point and his
only point.

The anti-divorce school seems strangely unable to recognize this positive conclusion, narrowly insisting that the qualification of "a good reputation" in Pauline teaching (1 Tim. 3:1, NIV, NASB) cannot be met by divorced-remarried persons. The very fact of divorce and remarriage in the past, they say, is tantamount to a bad reputation and reason enough for disqualification. But the problem with this reasoning is that it does not square with reality—at least not in our times. Divorce-and-remarriage does not automatically tag a person with a bad reputation. The question is really very straightforward: Does the good-reputation requirement preclude anyone previously divorced and remarried?

Bishops and elders, Paul teaches, are to be "above reproach," examples in all things (including monogamous marriage). They are to be men of good reputation. A practicing polygamist certainly would not have a good reputation. But what about the man who had a solid Christian marriage, a reputation for faithfulness to his wife—a model marriage in truth and in the eyes of the community—and yet some years past had been divorced and this was a remarriage? Does this status disqualify him from having a good reputation? Obviously not.

However true this might have been in the past, it is not so today, and this author knows of no evidence that it was a problem in Paul's day. On the contrary, in some instances a person's good reputation may have been earned by the very manner in which he or she recovered stability and grew to spiritual maturity through the trauma of divorce. All because the devastated individual appropriated God's healing grace and grew into a new obedience to His Word, into a closer walk with Him. I have known such individuals—especially victims of unwanted divorce. I have seen how carefully and prayerfully some have entered into a God-honoring remarriage, chastened and taught by the previous experience.

In this, as in so many of life's crises, what happens to a person is not the ultimate issue; what one does with what happens makes the difference. At some critical juncture one's positive reputation may be established in the eyes of the community, a reputation earned through triumphing over a terribly trying situation in a spiritually, emotionally, and cognitive way. This very reputation qualifies such a person for office in the church, for the most mature kind of service for Christ in the broken lives of His people.

Therefore, if a remarried person is not deemed worthy of official service, it then must be for reasons other than marital status as divorced-and-remarried—unless there remains attached to that status something immoral or otherwise unacceptable. It is the widely held opinion of our day that 1 Timothy 3:2 and Titus 1:6 do not disqualify persons from church office solely on the basis of their status as remarried after divorce.

With Gordon-Conwell theologian John Jefferson Davis, I concur: "The divorced person, through repentance, forgiveness, and the transforming presence of the Holy Spirit, may likewise transcend the failures of the past and win acceptance in the eyes of the God's people for a fruitful ministry of leadership and service."

We now move on to Part Three and grapple with some broader issues in the area of theological ethics. If we live as Christians under the ethic of the kingdom teachings of Jesus, as we surely do, how then does God apply this ethic to this time—when the kingdom is only spiritually present, and when kingdom ethics can only be partially fulfilled in the life of the church? What place does redemptive realism play in God's ethical governance of His church? How are kingdom ethics mediated by divine grace?

PART THREE

The Ruling
New Testament
Ethic of Grace
Applied to
Divorce and
Remarriage

7

Ethics for Fragile Saints

The final part of this book is designed to demonstrate how we arrive at our understanding of New Testament ethics within the special framework of grace. It provides the key to God's ethical governance in the church age, demonstrating how God deals with our imperfect attainment of kingdom ethics, especially how He deals with the reality of unwanted but unpreventable divorce and the normal prospect of remarriage.

The question of God's ethical governance in our time is not a simple matter, although fundamental to understanding many ethical issues. It is the old problem of "legalism versus grace." But within that dichotomy is a further question: *How do we translate the absolute norms of kingdom ethics, especially the Sermon on the Mount, into a workable ethic for fragile, failing saints?* A proper study of divorce must face this question.

What exactly do we find in the New Testament in terms of behavioral norms? Have we a single standard for righteous behavior? If so, and if kingdom ethics is that standard, as we believe, does this not simplify things? Does it not mean that either God approves or disapproves, and that is all there is to it? Not so! God's ethical governance takes into account many considerations. But the real problem is not the ethical

173

norms; it is our less-than-perfect fulfillment of them. We fail—sometimes inadvertently, at other times deliberately—all within our daily walk as earnest Christians. Our discipleship is sadly tarnished. At times we only partially understand what we are to do or not do—and why. Human ignorance, weakness, and sin take their toll in each of us. We have resources in Christ, yet we fail to draw upon them when we need them most. Our motivation to do what is right sometimes suffers because we are physically tired or mentally oppressed by the circumstances surrounding our lives. Or perhaps we are emotionally drained. Indeed, ethical conduct is conditioned by a wealth of human factors, some of them deep within our character. None of us lives a perfect, squeaky-clean Christian life.

We have heard it said that the ethical ideal is comprised of the "right, the good, and the beautiful." When it comes to God's perfect righteousness, these qualities abound—what is "right" according to His perfect standard, what is "good" according to His determination of the good, and what is "beautiful" according to His beautiful design. Against this ethical ideal we see the majesty of God's perfect righteousness defined for us in Jesus' kingdom ethics. Yet, as we set our sights upon fulfilling that righteousness, we despair that our conduct will ever reach those heights. Failing perfect fulfillment, what then? *Judgment or grace? Sanctions or new possibilities?* Until we can answer this question, our ethical understanding is only seeing in a glass darkly. Our conclusions regarding divorce and remarriage remain tentative.

The Kingdom and Its Righteousness

Our preliminary task is to outline the nature of the kingdom that Jesus promised and came to establish. To what extent is it being realized in the present age? How will it be fulfilled more completely in the age to come? Although the King and His kingdom were rejected by God's people Israel and the King banished from earth, the promise was not rescinded, only postponed. That kingdom remains the end toward which all history moves. This is the "eschatological" or end-time kingdom. Satan will then be bound, and the conditions of this world will reflect vast changes in preparation for the kingdom's establishment. Then the King will return to reign personally in the power of His glorious presence, all conditions conducive to righteousness.

The futurity of the kingdom makes the church age unique. It is an interim period. The kingdom has gone underground, as it were. What is crucial to our study of the ethics of divorce is that the kingdom ethic is presently in effect in its perfection, yet is attainable only to a limited extent. This interim age is marked by human weakness and failure, by intrusive sin, by pressures from a godless world, by Satan's assaults. Christians are caught up in non-kingdom surroundings. *The Epistles make it perfectly evident that the church on earth is made up of struggling saints who are capable of sin and failure.* The record of ethical attainment for Christians is at best marred and incomplete. Even the most dedicated groups of believers cannot claim perfect obedience. How does God administer His perfect righteousness under these conditions? Is His moral governance of necessity provisional in some respect? He cannot compromise His moral absolutes, nor can He wink at our disobedience. Where there is failure, such as divorce, does God meet us in judgment and prohibitions, or does He provide for our recovery, whether within the broken marital bond or outside it? Tough questions! How grateful we are, knowing that we are cradled within the redemptive realism that is the gospel!

Perfect Future—But Limited Present

Our initial task, then, is to outline the parameters of the kingdom in its present and future forms. To what extent is the absolute ethic of the future kingdom realizable in the present? Our course of study may seem circuitous at this point, but it is essential if we are to get our ethical bearings sufficiently to deal unambiguously with the specific issue of divorce and remarriage as a question of theological ethics.

An observation that most writers on the subject of divorce and remarriage seem to miss is that the recorded words of Jesus are set within His teaching concerning kingdom righteousness, at least in two of the four accounts. This is a special context. The kingdom is the major theme, the overriding theme, of the synoptic Gospels. The continuity of both Testaments lies in the kingdom prophesied in the Psalms and Prophets, offered by the King who came and who, according to the historical record of the New Testament, was rejected by God's people Israel. This rejection delayed the establishment of the kingdom upon earth. During the church age, the kingdom is present in hidden form, the King present spiritually among His people. The ethical norms of the kingdom are adapted to God's governance of a people redeemed but struggling in a world that owns not the King. During this period, God is redemptively at work, establishing the church as a body of believers united to Him through His spiritual presence. The written Word of God is their external guide, the indwelling Holy Spirit their inward Guide and enabling power. Although the church represents the kingdom and manifests its characteristics, the church is not identical with the kingdom. The church administers a pre-kingdom rule on behalf of the absent King. In that coming day, Christian believers will participate in the kingdom in its fullness. That kingdom will be characterized by perfect righteousness under the personal rule of the no-longer-absent King. It will be a righteous, peaceful, and just society governed by kingdom ethics. No longer will Satan be the god of this world, as he is now by God's sovereign sufferance. Kingdom ethics in their absolute form, designed for that reign of righteousness, are suited to higher possibilities of human fulfillment than can be effected during this interim church age. This is not to say that we are not subject to such righteousness; we are indeed. This is our only standard. By the enabling ministry of the Holy Spirit, we seek earnestly to live a righteous life to the glory of our God and Savior. *Fulfillment is our goal.*

We have a glimpse of kingdom ethics fulfilled in the life and ministry of Jesus. He Himself was the reality of the kingdom. He Himself was the righteousness and perfection demanded of the citizens of the kingdom. His public ministry was both a demonstration of and a call to the kingdom. All that Jesus did was consistent with the absolutes of perfect kingdom righteousness.

The synoptic Gospels—Matthew, Mark, and Luke—form the historical transition from the Old Covenant to the New. As we noted in the confrontation of Jesus with the Pharisees, He was teaching the true requirements of Old Testament law. However, the burden of His message was not the law and its reinterpretation but the true righteousness that would succeed the law, the righteousness of His kingdom.

We recall how God summoned Israel to be the people of His rule; He entered into irrevocable covenants with them. Their disobedience and consequent judgment could not cancel out God's purpose or reverse His covenants. But it did allow men's failings to bring about a delay in the final enactment of God, the establishment of the Messianic kingdom. It brought about a postponement. But with the postponement came an interim pre-form of the kingdom in the birth of the church.

For the prophets, the "day of the Lord" was both a direct act of God expected in history and God's ultimate earthly visitation. The prophets did not distinguish between these two aspects but viewed them as one and the same. They were not given to see the two advents of Christ with an interim between. As members of the body of Christ, the church—looking back upon His death and return to heaven, yet forward to His return to establish His kingdom—we are in position to understand the place and purpose of the interim. God's redemptive work continues on. We conclude with George Eldon Ladd that the tension between the future and the present is the tension between the kingdom in complete future consummation and the kingdom breaking in upon the present order in partial fulfillment. This tension is the key to the ethical dilemma that calls forth the mediating grace of God—His governance of the church age through redemptive, renewing grace.

Grace Makes Its Entrance

To some extent there is a commingling of grace principles in Jesus' kingdom teaching, but this is left undeveloped. There is little more than anticipation of the age of grace. It is in John's Gospel and especially in the Epistles that grace principles make full entrance. The Epistles are not directly concerned with the offer of the kingdom or with the kingdom ethic as set forth in the synoptic Gospels. The emphasis shifts from the specifics of kingdom righteousness to the Christian's personal growth in conformity to Jesus Christ, his relinquishing the old and taking on the new. The Synoptics reveal their complexity, however, as they set forth a composite picture not easily sorted out. First, Jesus interprets Mosaic law; second, He teaches kingdom righteousness; third, He addresses the nation that is rejecting Him and His righteousness; fourth, He speaks in parables to teach the hidden form of the kingdom during this age. *Finally,* Jesus gives glimpses of grace principles in terms of God's present governance of His people. This is the least developed of these several themes. To sort this out and give proper place to God's governance through grace is the task of a well-developed contextual approach. It is for this reason that we are carefully outlining the differences in ethical contexts.

Interestingly, there is no record in the synoptic Gospels of movement toward the church's formation until Jesus' rejection has become an irreversible reality. In covenant faithfulness, God did not set aside His promise of the kingdom. *The church interim is representative of and preparatory to that kingdom to come.*

During the days of His ministry to Israel, Jesus endorsed Mosaic legislation but not the interpretation given by the scribes and Pharisees. At the same time He introduced new principles to be applied in the kingdom as "these sayings of mine." It was not until the upper-room discourse that He revealed these new principles, which were to govern the church, the "new creation." Kingdom righteousness is no longer demanded in an unqualified sense. For an imperfect church, God's governance becomes provisional. *The ethic remains intact, while grace becomes the operational principle.* It is God's transcendant way of ministering to human inability. Here bright hope reaches beyond defeat and despair—the hope of renewing grace!

The Mystery of the Kingdom

From the moment of His official rejection, Christ's ministry took on the nature of preparation for an interim. It is very apparent from the narrative that a wholly new epoch in our Lord's ministry had now begun. He turned to parables whose purpose was to reveal to the disciples truths concealed from the rejecting and rejected nation Israel. The disciples were genuine citizens of the kingdom yet to come. At the same time they were members of the church, which represents the kingdom and displays its powers in the present age. To them Jesus said, "To you it has been given to know the secrets of the kingdom of heaven, but to them it has not been given" (Matt. 13:11).

The mystery of the kingdom is the coming of the King into history in advance of its apocalyptic manifestation. To be sure, it is a partial albeit genuine in-breaking of the kingdom. This is the single truth illustrated by the several parables in Matthew 13. The kingdom, which comes in apocalyptic power in the end-time, has in fact entered the world in hidden form to work secretly among men. This was an utterly novel idea, for the Old Testament nowhere gave so much as an intimation of this mystery.

Be sure of this—the present aspect of the kingdom in mystery form does not replace the expected kingdom nor modify it in any way. It supplements it, giving it a pre-form. The church exists only because there was a rejection and postponement of the kingdom. This is not to suggest that the church was not in the predetermined plan of God, since in His sovereign purpose and foreknowledge, each stage in the unfolding kingdom was perfectly known and planned. Both future and present are encompassed within His eternal purpose. *The present ethical governance by grace was already there in the predetermined plan of God.*

Time Between the Times

When rejection of both King and His kingdom was sealed beyond any possible reversal, Jesus announced the birth of the church—not as something He had been building all along or was then building. And although the church is not the kingdom, it represents the kingdom at this time. To the church was given "the keys of the kingdom of heaven" (Matt. 16:19). To the church was given a specific authority for an appointed time and a mission to these times. *Thus the church plays a twofold role: an interim role that is simultaneously a preparatory role.*

Those who are brought to salvation in this age become citizens of the future kingdom. Moreover, they are kingdom citizens now. They experience the quality of kingdom rule and righteousness, as it were, in advance form. The very life of the King is theirs by the indwelling Holy Spirit, the life-directing Word of the King is theirs in the written Scripture, and the powers of the King are theirs for ministry as well. This is brought out in Colossians 1:13: "He has delivered us from the dominion of darkness and transferred us to the kingdom of his beloved Son." Here we have an accomplished fact, a present reality. Our position as believers in Christ means that we are citizens of His kingdom now, citizens in a pre-form of the kingdom yet to come.

Let us be perfectly clear about the dual nature of the kingdom. Because the kingdom has not come in fullness, and cannot until the King Himself returns to take up His worldwide reign, this is in no way tantamount to there being no present kingdom reality, that there can be no pre-form of the kingdom beforehand. Not at all. Where the King is, there is the kingdom; where the King is present, there He reigns. The kingdom is here now in terms of the King's rule in the lives of His redeemed subjects—a spiritual reign. Yet the kingdom is not here now in its full consummation, when, as we expect, the King's rule over earth will be complete and undisputed.

It is here that Scripture forces a disclaimer upon us. While we as the King's subjects are given all the resources of Word and Spirit to fulfill the kingdom ethics, perfect right-eousness can only be imperfectly achieved in the church age. The powers of the world, the flesh, and the devil con-spire against the believer. It has always been a struggling church, and it always will be until Jesus comes. It lives through victories and defeats, sometimes taking steps for-ward, sometimes backward, yet always moving ahead confi-dently in the continuing experience of God's renewing grace and power.

As we might expect, since the three synoptic Gospels have so much to do with Jesus' ministry, His rejection and death, and all that lay ahead, these Gospels unite their tes-timony regarding the glorious return of Christ to establish His kingdom, thus climaxing the end-time. John's Gospel has a different emphasis. He gives attention to the last hours of Jesus' ministry, hours spent in intimate instruc-tion of the disciples who shall carry on after His departure. These themes largely concern the present church interim. John is more concerned to prepare the disciples for this pe-riod, especially that they might know Jesus in His spiritual presence, no longer in His physical presence. In Jesus' won-derful prayer, which follows immediately after the upper-room discourse, the emphasis is upon the disciples' being kept from the evil one (John 17:15). That prayer envisions the disciples as living and working in the harassing envi-ronment of Satan's kingdom. Suffering and persecution lie ahead. There will be many difficult experiences facing the church. Life will not run smoothly and perfectly, nor will sin and failure be eradicated from the body of Christ on earth. Moral and spiritual lapses will recur. For some, these lapses will surface in the form of marital breakup, although John's Gospel does not point to this specifically.

It is apparent that the difficulties Christians face, including the marital, arise from the fact that the kingdom of Christ presently runs parallel with the kingdom of Satan, and there are intertwining features that can cause even the most mature believer to stumble and fail. We are a vulnerable people.

How shall the church adapt to this partial manifestation of the kingdom? This, too, is not the burden of the synoptic Gospels but of John and the Epistles. Failures to fulfill kingdom righteousness within the church must eventuate either in some form of judgment or in the provisional action of forgiving, renewing grace. This is precisely the case with marriage breakup. It may bring in its wake some difficult consequences, sometimes a struggle with deserved guilt. Where is the heart of God? With sanctions against the failing ones—or with renewing grace that holds out new possibilities and new commitments? Here we affirm the transcendance of grace in God's moral governance of His church.

The church's mission is to witness to the kingdom and its principles of righteous living. That witness has its greatest impact as the church lives out those principles before the eyes of non-Christians, demonstrating the higher call of God. Whenever a successful Christian marriage continues over time, growing in covenant integrity, there is a unique witness to the world that Christ makes the difference. But we must not minimize the secondary witness that is possible in the face of marital breakup. Sometimes the witness is to a remarkable reconciliation. How wonderfully reassuring this can be! Gratefully, this occurs again and again! At other times there is witness to God's forgiving and renewing grace, to the enduring commitment and fidelity of a second marriage. We cannot deny that there is more than one way in which God's power and grace can be witnessed.

It is not always in a first success! We must remember that grace is God's way of mediating between His perfect will and our imperfect response. *The ultimate issue of divorce and remarriage finds its resolution in the arena of God's forgiving, renewing grace.*

8

Living in the Interim

We have now introduced a number of working concepts in our study of New Testament ethics. This approach was taken so that we can look at last at divorce and remarriage with a well-thought-through basis in theological ethics. We should find ourselves better able to take a mature biblical position, then move on to either the ministry that faces us or to personal decisions, as the case may be.

We have begun to see the nature of the kingdom to be established when the King returns, how it broke into history in advance when the king came in His first advent. The kingdom is present in the church today in believers whose lives are committed to Him and indwelt by the Holy Spirit. The church represents the kingdom during this age and demonstrates its powers and hopes. Believers are citizens of that coming kingdom while now living in an interim time, a pre-form of the kingdom. *Especially important to our study, is that the ethics of the kingdom are in effect during this interim, but absolute attainment is not possible.* In our striving to fulfill these ethical demands, we have a precious provision in the forgiving, renewing grace of a loving God. We now ask two related questions: In what way does God administer kingdom righteousness in our time? How does grace mediate between God's perfect way and our imperfect attainment? This is the issue we continue to pursue.

185

Men as diverse as E. F. Scott and Paul Ramsey concur that Jesus' kingdom ethic was totally conditioned by eschatology—concern for end-time events. He set forth the will of God for life in that coming kingdom. Eldon Ladd summarizes by saying that if Jesus' ethics are in fact the ethics of the reign of God, it follows that they must be absolute ethics. He affirms the insight of Martin Dibelius that Jesus taught the pure, unconditional will of God without compromise of any sort. God lays His unconditional will upon man for all time. That perfect will is attainable only in the age to come, when all evil has been banished. But it is also quite clear from the Sermon on the Mount that Jesus expected His disciples to practice His teachings in this present age, even as they anticipated the coming kingdom. What was not generally understood until recent times is that the kingdom has entered history without transforming history. And now, during this time of waiting, we have an imperfect church, readily confessing its imperfection yet pointing ever to the incredible grace of God. Nothing delights our God more than mending broken lives and restoring men and women to new possibilities. By grace He restores the equilibrium of life when things go wrong.

History Divided by Two Aeons

A masterful way of envisioning all this is provided by the German theologian Helmut Thielicke. He speaks of the "Old Aeon" and the "New Aeon." The Old Aeon represents the fallen world, the reign of Satan and sin. This period of history extends from the fall of man to the second advent of Christ and the establishment of His kingdom on earth. The New Aeon represents the kingdom in its present and future reality, covering the period from the first Advent of Christ to the eternal state. The thing we must grasp about the two aeons is that they do not follow one after the other, the new succeeding the old. Rather, they overlap: the Old Aeon continues on to the second advent of Christ, but the New Aeon already began earlier at the first advent of Christ. For a period of time, both aeon's are present at once, overlapping the span of time from the first to the second advents of Christ. Christians are living in this interim, this overlapping period; their lives are touched by both aeons.

We see the unique place the interim occupies; the church age incorporates elements of both Old Aeon and New. To govern this interim God accordingly has an interim ethic. It is the kingdom ethic, but because of the present impossibility of that ethic's being perfectly achieved, it is a perfect ethic mediated by grace. This is possible within God's provisional will, and it is this possibility that shapes our thinking about divorce and remarriage. See figure 1 to help visualize this concept.

Jesus said we are in the world but not of it. Translated into Thielicke's concept, we are in the Old Aeon but not of it. We are citizens of the New Aeon, the kingdom. Still, we are not able to attain perfect righteousness. What keeps us from subsequent despair is that redemptive grace continually intervenes to restore our potential for living in the fullness of God's blessing. *In His loving purpose there are always new beginnings!*

As a form of God's rule, the interim church age is distinct unto itself. It is neither the former Mosaic administration of theocratic law, nor the kingdom administration of theocratic law. The church is governed by kingdom ethics mediated by grace. For the most part, Christian living is guided by appeals to be like Jesus, to live as He instructs. The church is not a theocratic kingdom; it is in the world yet not of it—or over it! The church was not created to rule society in this evil age. The kingdom of Satan and the kingdoms of this world must give way before the kingdom of our Lord Jesus Christ is established. The church is, in fact, an alien subculture within the social structures of this world. It is no more than a beachhead of the kingdom of God.

Satan is called "the god of this world" (2 Cor. 4:4). He introduces disorder into human life in ways that affect Christian men and women individually and in their relationships. As God's people do not yet live in the king-

Figure 1   **The Relationship Between the Two Aeons**

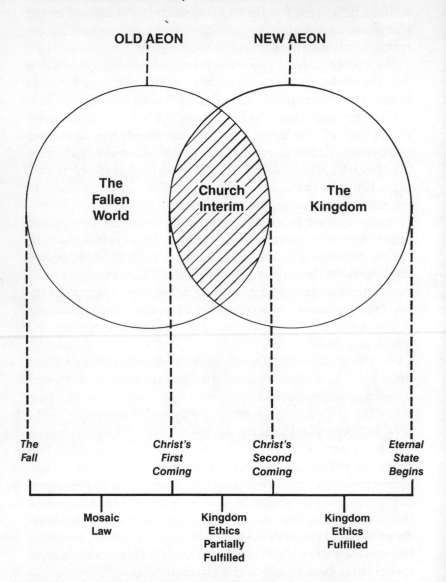

This scheme holds true regardless of one's particular millennial view. *Premillennialists* are divided over the time of the church's rapture, but the overlapping period is still essentially the same. *Amillennialists* identify the millennium with the kingdom, yet recognize that the Old Aeon ends with Christ's return, hence an overlapping period.

dom, neither do they live according to a perfectly established ethic. Apart from the supporting conditions of the
kingdom, God's people can only make an imperfect response. Conditions of the Old Aeon, as we have seen, shall
prevail throughout the entire church interim. Therefore, in
every age the church struggles for its life in the world, and
believers suffer the conflicts and contradictions of this life.

Our personal sanctification as believers is attained in dif-
fering degrees. No two Christians attain exactly the same
maturity in Christ. Growth into the likeness of Jesus Christ
is a gradual, progressive maturation in the Spirit. As Christians differ in their knowledge of God's will and ability to
appropriate the resources available to them in Christ, inevitably there will be degrees of failure in attaining the
kingdom's ethical demands. There continues to be conflict
between the flesh and the Spirit (Gal. 5:16–24). As described
in Romans 7, the regenerated person delights in the law of
God with his mind but finds another law at war against this
law. His continuing problem is that the conditions of the Old
Aeon alter the possibility of his fully implementing the ethical demands of the New. For some people, understandably,
their less-than-successful effort centers in marriage. More
often than we could wish, there results in time an unwanted
but unpreventable divorce.

Attainable Yet Unattainable

At best, Christians can only approximate the ideal.
Christ's own people are inextricably bound to the ethics of
conflict and compromise, for this is the only world we know.
It necessitates an ethics built on forgiving, renewing grace.
At times our situation requires a moral choice between two
things, both good. At other times our dilemma is the tragic
moral choice we must make between the lesser of two evils.
Every Christian faces this less-than-ideal reality in one
area of life or another. The New Testament knows nothing of
perfectionism, despite the perfect ethic it puts before us.
This certainly means that perfection cannot be expected

in the sphere of marriage. Realistically, we expect some couples to stumble in this most critical and demanding of human relationships. But are they singled out to remain in their failure?

All too painfully are we reminded of our continuity with the Old Aeon—succumbing at times to the sins that easily beset us, coming short so often in living the Christian life according to our own expectations, not to speak of God's. But there is a glorious discontinuity as well; believers are constantly being delivered from this evil age as they grow in Christ and in the power of the Holy Spirit. Of course, this means making spiritual choices. It also means a spiritually disciplined lifestyle. Success invariably takes place in the lives of those who spend time in God's Word and in the discipline of prayer, who walk with the Lord in trust and obedience, and who choose to turn away from the alluring and deceiving call of worldly values—especially as they assault Christian values of marriage fidelity.

Discontinuity with the New Aeon is painfully and equally evident on every side, as we reach for the powers of the kingdom only to find they cannot be fully ours at present. We are severely limited.

Christian ethics, as Thielicke points out, is concerned with the church's ensconcement in the Old Aeon. God wills that the fallen, passing world be the environment in which we Christians live out our lives in the Spirit. There is a cosmic struggle that touches all human life in this world, since Satan is still an unbridled antagonist. Although the risen, ascended Christ is Victor, He has not yet taken up His victory on earth. We share His victory now in real and dynamic ways—but incompletely.

The paradox of New Testament ethics for Christians is that the righteousness of the kingdom is both attainable and unattainable. It is attainable in part, not in fullness—attainable in certain ways by some individuals, not by others. In this sense it remains "the impossible possibility." We grow in conformity to our Lord and accumulate victories over sin, yet all the while we deeply long for that day when we shall be made whole, fully delivered from sin, self, and the fallen age. Then we shall attain, though now only in part.

Life as a Field of Tension

Christian ethics adapts itself to life as a field of tension, the tension that exists between the Old and New Aeons. There is a sense in which we are all trapped in this field of tension. Nor is it possible to resolve the tension by all our attempts to fulfill kingdom righteousness. Instead, Christian ethics enables us to walk in both worlds, to live within the tension, to grow in personal responsiveness to the Spirit. We are never brought to the place in this life where we are released from this tension. So long as life lasts, no Christian shall live either above or apart from this field of tension. It is only by God's grace that we escape the pitfalls we do. We have only the victories that God enables us to win along the way. Our confidence, however, is that what God requires of us He makes possible in Christ, and all the while His arms of grace are there to catch us when we fall.

How vastly superior is this assurance in contrast with the notion that God is inflexible in His rule, that forgiveness is not accompanied by restoring grace, that failure will forever remove us from His favor or from the possibility of a new beginning. What a world of difference lies between the approach to a biblical ethics that is inflexible law, and the approach through creative love and renewing grace! Redemptive possibilities are always the outcome of grace transcendent—*marriage not excepted.*

When we attempt to deny all justification of divorce, we end with "If only. . . ." We say, "If only you had tried harder. If only you had prayed more earnestly. If only you had trusted God for a miracle. If only you had more faith. If only you were more loving, more patient. If only you were not so self-centered. If only you had been in the Word more. If only you had taken those six counseling sessions with the pastor." It all sounds as though Job's miserable counselors have been outdone!

It is only when we stop trying to deny the reality of divorce and the appropriate occasions for it that we can be helpful. This includes willingness to relate personally to those who have suffered. We can deplore what has happened, while at the same time understanding it. Better still, we can love the suffering persons.

Sanctification and the Rule of Grace

The Christian is ever in the process of "putting off the old man" (see Eph. 4:1–2; Col. 3:9). Our sanctification is a progressive putting off of the old nature and putting on the new, of gradual conformity to the likeness of our Lord. Although new creatures in Christ, Christians are in the continual process of being delivered from the power of the unredeemed within themselves. Pride of self, passions of the flesh, envy and jealousy, bitterness and hatred—these and many other areas—remain to be subjected to the sanctifying grace of Christ. In other words, Christians are always in the process of "becoming"—becoming what they *are* in Christ.

Perhaps the most remarkable passage of Scripture in this entire regard is Ephesians 2:7: "That in the coming ages he might show the immeasurable riches of his grace in kindness toward us in Christ Jesus." Evidently there is to be a mighty demonstration before all the inhabitants of God's cosmic realm, a demonstration of divine grace in all its richness. The object will be not only the multitude saved by grace, but these "immeasurable riches" will include the church's struggle, its victories and defeats.

Think, too, of Paul's classic statement on the rule of grace:

For the grace of God has appeared for the salvation of all men, training us to renounce irreligion and worldly passions, and to live sober, upright, and godly lives in this world, awaiting our blessed hope, the appearing of the glory of our great God and Savior Jesus Christ, who gave himself for us to redeem us from all iniquity and to purify for himself a people of his own who are zealous for good deeds. (Titus 2:11–14).

Here we have the basic elements of the New Testament rule of grace. Our growth comes not as a matter of coercion by inflexible law but through training in righteousness. We do certain things and not others, not in order to comply with rules, but that our lives might rise in ever-greater conformity to God's own holy nature. Growth is gradual, not instantaneous, but for many the years show anything but a great degree of growth in the life of the Spirit. Yet how different is this from a legalistic ethic, which imposes a demand for perfect attainment and threatens us with heavy sanctions and prohibitions if we fail. The purpose of the Holy Spirit's ministry in our lives is not to produce perfect lawkeepers as such, but men and women increasingly sensitive to sin, increasingly subject to God and His will, increasingly manifesting growth in likeness to Jesus both within and without. Listen to Paul in Romans 6:15–18. Here he puts it on the line:

What then? Are we to sin because we are not under law but under grace? By no means! Do you not know that if you yield yourselves to any one as obedient slaves, you are slaves of the one whom you obey, either of sin, which leads to death, or of obedience, which leads to righteousness? But thanks be to God, that you who were once slaves of sin have become obedient from the heart to the standard of teaching to which you were committed, and, having been set free from sin, have become slaves of righteousness.

There is no instantaneous or fast route to Christian maturity offered here. But the essential point is that grace does not invite presumptuousness. Grace is the great incentive to live for the smile of the One who is gracious to us. Those who fear that grace will lead to presumptuousness fail to reckon with the nature and power of grace or with the convicting ministry of the Holy Spirit. It is grace that inwardly impels the Christian to live so as to please the Giver of grace. How different is this from obeying out of fear of punishment! Grace plants the desire for holiness in our hearts. What a range of ministry there is in God's gifts of grace. Grace is the most powerful of all incentives!

Redemptive Realism
Shall Prevail at Last

This is the glorious message to the church today. Where, actually, can the church point to ethical perfection within its life in the world? Nowhere. And surely, if not elsewhere, then not in the most intimate, demanding relationship of all—marriage. Rather, the church is called to exercise the same grace toward marital failure that God exercises toward whatever other failures His children suffer. We simply must acknowledge the potential for Christians to fail. Failure is a part of human growth.

There is one further dimension to all this. While we would be careful not to blame Satan for our own failings, we cannot ignore the fact that he is constantly aiming to frustrate the working of kingdom principles among God's people. We cannot underestimate Satan's power or his wiles. But if we will trust God and obey Him, "... greater is he that is in you, than he that is in the world" (I John 4:4, KJV). The Spirit within us holds the key to victory, whether in strictly personal matters or in relational matters such as marriage.

In such critical concerns as divorce and remarriage, it is really to the God of all grace that we look for guidance. In Him we place all our confidence, resting in His creative love and grace. That grace is sufficient for our every need, whatever that need may be. If it is for the restoration of a deteriorating marriage—and restoration is His highest and best—He will then do the extraordinary, whatever it takes. If in His eyes the situation is irremediably destructive and truly without promise for the future, the appeal is still to His restorative grace. He knows what is best, all things considered. He cares about what our best interests are in the long run. In His foreknowledge He may have in view a healing, fulfilling, God-honoring second marriage; this may indeed be His highest provision of grace. If so, then who are we to back off from this possibility for someone whose situation we cannot possibly know in depth and hence cannot fully or perhaps correctly judge?

The bottom line is that God has given us a perfect ethical ideal. However—in terms of our corporate needs as His church today and in terms of His loving governance of His church—it is an ideal mediated by grace. But do not make the mistake of underestimation; in the exercise of His grace God is glorified in one of His highest, most precious attributes. And through the exercise of His grace we experience the wonder of creative love!

9

Goals and Ideals

Jesus' declaration about divorce and remarriage in the fifth chapter of Matthew has special significance for the reason that it comes within that incomparable body of teaching known as the Sermon on the Mount. It is thus a part of the highest ethical mandate to come from the lips of Jesus. The Sermon on the Mount is set forth as a set of laws and placed in contrast with Mosaic laws. It is such an intensified interpretation of Mosaic law that it is commonly called a radicalized form. *In a very real sense we may regard this as God's ultimate ethical law for His people.* Here is the Manifesto of the King, the moral and social mandate of the kingdom of God. It authenticates Jesus' kingly authority and demonstrates the ultimacy of kingdom law and its transcendence over Mosaic law. Jesus shows that he stands above the law given by Moses. A student of the Sermon must be careful to note that one-third of it is dominated by eschatology—matters relating to the end-time, to the consummation of the messianic kingdom. This very characteristic cautions us at once to see that it is about perfect righteousness designed for that perfect kingdom yet to come.

Let me illustrate. Kingdom righteousness is here related to the law as the Jews knew it through Moses. Six examples

197

show how Jesus interprets the law in terms of true righteousness. Each example opens with the words—always the
same formula—"You have heard it said." Then, in each instance, Jesus adds, "But I say to you." Then He proceeds to
show how the law is elevated to totally new requirements in
the kingdom. We will examine this a bit further on.

Redemptive Ends Not in View

Curiously, the first thing to stand out is that Jesus does
not introduce into the Sermon any redemptive means to
meet the possible failure of His people to fulfill the Sermon's imperatives. His is a word of judgment only, severe
judgment at that. Not a hint of grace appears in the entire
Sermon. Jesus makes the leap from Mosaic governance to
kingdom governance without disclosing His purpose in
redemptive grace at all. That teaching, so familiar to us, is
found elsewhere.

The divorce-and-remarriage passage (Matt. 5:31–32)
makes up one of these six examples of radicalized law. It,
too, speaks to the superior righteousness of the kingdom.
How this absolute applies to the church of the interim is our
fundamental concern. But first we need to get our bearings
with reference to the nature of the Sermon itself.

Our Relationship to
Ethical Absolutes

A further impression from just surveying the Sermon is
that here we have ethical perfectionism quite beyond all
present human capability. We are compelled to assume that
what is beyond human capability is also beyond divine expectation (if we confine our consideration to the present
church age). If we isolate the Sermon from the rest of New
Testament ethics, we have to agree with Hans Windisch:
"The religion of the Sermon on the Mount is predominantly
a religion of works." This conclusion results from noting

that there is not a word about saving grace or forgiveness for failure—only judgment. Nor is there a word about the Holy Spirit's enabling believers to fulfill this ultimate ethical mandate. For reasons not easily detected, Jesus limits His words to the defining of perfect righteousness. Windisch is led to say, "There is a gulf here between Jesus and Paul that no art of theological exegesis can bridge."

But wait! If Jesus is addressing the ethic of the coming perfect kingdom, the gulf is bridged, and we do have a solution to the enigma. The ethic is mediated by grace in an age when perfect fulfillment is not possible. And besides, it does apply to the church today, since these ethical absolutes constitute the ideal, not law. We do seek to fulfill the ideal as the Spirit empowers us, and this is the goal of Christian living. Yet we know that for us the ideal contains no threat of judgment for failure, only God's mediating grace. This is the ethic governing the church interim!

Jesus is pictured here as the new Moses, declaring a new law. The Sermon with its absolutes envisions a righteousness demanded by the pure will of God. Hear the summary: "For I tell you, unless your righteousness exceeds that of the scribes and Pharisees, you will never enter the kingdom of heaven" (Matt. 5:20). What puzzles Christians, saved by grace apart from works of righteousness, is this apparent declaration that entrance into the kingdom of heaven is indeed by means of superior personal righteousness. How do we put this into proper perspective?

It is as though Jesus were saying, "You talk of attaining righteousness by the law of Moses; I'm telling you of the true righteousness of God, which supersedes the law of Moses. The righteousness of Messiah's kingdom is righteousness in the inner as well as outer life. It concerns heart and mind, attitudes and dispositions—what motivates a person's actions. It is no less than perfect, as God is perfect. If a person would claim righteousness for himself, righteousness that entitles him to enter the kingdom of God, he must be as righteous as God, for there is no righteousness on a lesser standard. So, if a person would come to God on the basis of his own righteousness, *let him be assured that God accepts nothing less than perfect righteousness. And to know what that is, I am giving you some of its principles."*

Now, clearly, we do not and cannot come to God upon the basis of our own righteousness, but only upon the righteousness of Christ, the righteousness He imputes to us, having made it ours through His atoning death and resurrection. It becomes ours upon the basis of faith alone, not by human merit.

Interestingly, there is nothing comparable to this teaching of the Sermon on the Mount in the Epistles, which were written to direct the life of the church. Thus, if we are to relate the message of the Sermon to the grace principles of the Epistles, we must locate the bridge that spans the two. This we have already done, we hope to the reader's satisfaction. That bridge is the interim church with its interim ethical governance, by which God meets our imperfect attainment of righteousness with His forgiving, renewing grace.

To cap the whole essence of Jesus' sayings in the Sermon, listen to the closing, "You, therefore, must be perfect, as your heavenly Father is perfect" (Matt. 5:48). And although various interpreters have sought to attach different meanings to the word, it does mean "perfect." In fact, the Father's being perfect is just that and nothing less! Since no person can make personal claim to this perfect righteousness, how and when is the mandate fulfilled?

It is unavoidable; Jesus says that His kingdom shall be governed by perfect righteousness, including fulfillment of the marriage mandate. Yet this is not possible during the church age. True, we have the uncompromised standard for righteous living, the absolutes. Yet the church cannot attain to these absolutes. What then? The church aims for these absolutes as ideals, as the highest motivation for Christian living as the Spirit grants the enablement. The church succeeds in degrees, sometimes to a very high degree; the rest is left with God's grace.

Contrasting Principles

What a different world we enter as we read, say, the words of Paul that "he saved us, not because of deeds done by us in righteousness, but in virtue of his own mercy, by the washing of regeneration and renewal in the Holy Spirit" (Titus 3:6). The Sermon on the Mount is not about mercy, justification by faith, or the washing of regeneration and renewal in the Holy Spirit. And neither does the Sermon give any hint of God's provisional will; its focus is not upon the redemptive aspects of our faith.

It is a curious thing that those who insist upon taking Jesus' word on divorce and remarriage from the Sermon on the Mount, without any qualification, are silent when it comes to the other demands of the Sermon and their consequences. Let us just read the portion of the Sermon that forms the immediate context of the divorce-and-remarriage statement:

> [Jesus said:] "You have heard that it was said to the men of old, 'You shall not kill; and whoever kills shall be liable to judgment.' But I say to you that everyone who is angry with his brother shall be liable to judgment; whoever insults his brother shall be liable to the council, and whoever says, 'You fool!' shall be liable to the hell of fire. . . . You have heard that it was said, 'You shall not commit adultery.' But I say to you that every one who looks at a woman lustfully has already committed adultery with her in his heart. If your right eye causes you to sin, pluck it out and throw it away. . . . It was also said, 'Whoever divorces his wife, let him give her a certificate of divorce.' But I say to you that every one who divorces his wife, except on the ground of unchastity, makes her an adulteress; and whoever marries a divorced woman commits adultery." (Matt. 5:21–22, 27–29, 31–32).

Did you note just how radicalized these statements are? Anyone who gets angry with another is liable to judgment! Anyone who looks lustfully at a woman is guilty of adultery!

How do you handle that? How often do you hear sermons telling of the judgment you will incur by getting angry or looking lustfully or calling another a name? Do you really think it true that you will be liable to the fire of hell for these offenses? No, of course not. But why? Because you are not trusting your own righteousness to keep you from hell. You are not fearful of God's condemning you on the basis of imperfect righteousness. You are saved by grace from all judgment, from all penalty. You stand on Romans 8:1: "There is therefore now no condemnation for those who are in Christ Jesus." Jesus took all your judgment at Calvary; you are righteous in Christ.

Marriage in the Radicalized Ethic

Now let us be consistent. We must see the divorce-and-remarriage statements in the same light as these other radicalized statements. In such a radicalized, absolute ethic, we must be surprised that Jesus conceded even a single exception, that of adultery! The message is that if we are presently bound by such an absolute ethic as this—perfect kingdom righteousness—there is then no other justifiable cause for divorce than adultery. But, in the church interim, our relation to perfect kingdom righteousness is as goal and ideal. Since we have the knowledge of the highest, we can make that our dedicated aim. We, too, desire nothing less than the highest divine standard. In our love for the Lord Jesus Christ, we want nothing less than what He wants. But to keep it all in realistic perspective, we need the ethic of forgiving, renewing grace, which the Epistles add to our understanding of the Sermon.

We cannot emphasize too strongly that kingdom law expressed in the radicalized ethic of the Sermon on the Mount is absolutely unyielding. For example, "Judge not, that you be not judged. For with the judgment you pronounce you will be judged, and the measure you give will be the measure you get" (Matt. 7:1–2). Yet the Christian, positioned in Christ, has passed beyond judgment. Of course, there is the future judgment seat Paul tells us is a judgment for rewards, but this is not the same as sin being returned in the form of judgment. Moreover, for the Christian, confession is the way to forgiveness and cleansing (1 John 1:9). How very different this is from the imperatives of the Sermon, which concludes with warnings and the ominous word that only the most dedicated and obedient will attain the way that leads to life (Matt. 7:13–27).

God's Conditional Will

We speak somewhat paradoxically of God's absolute ethical imperatives, this being His "unconditional will" as He designed it for a humanity created in His image and likeness, a humanity then able to live it. At the same time, we speak of God's "conditional will," whereby he administers His righteous will in accommodation to mankind's fallen state. This accommodation extends throughout the history of God's ethical governance of His people. His present will is provisional toward those who, having sinned, meet His conditions of penitence and commit themselves to moving on in obedience to Him. His will is provisional in that He provides forgiving, restoring grace. Ultimately, it is only as we accept the theological legitimacy of God's conditional, provisional will in a fallen world that we can fully grasp the truth of His governance of His people by grace. This truth is the centerpiece of New Testament ethics. Furthermore, it is the principle by which we judge any system claiming to teach Christian ethics.

With the new mandates of kingdom ethics, God also provides new means for compliance through the empowerment of the Holy Spirit. To both guide and enable God's people is an essential function of the indwelling Spirit of God. If believers were to place their lives completely under the Spirit's control, kingdom ethics would be perfectly attainable in all respects. One problem sometimes ignored is spiritual immaturity, a major disability when it comes to placing marriage under the Spirit's control. It takes both partners to subject marriage successfully to God's standards and to the Spirit's control. This accounts for much marital breakdown.

Is it not strange how prone we are to judge and condemn those whose marriages have ended, all the while ignoring the defeats Christians exhibit with reference to other mandates of the Sermon? Is it because we struggle with marital problems of our own, which threaten to undo us, that we experience some degree of relief as we look judgmentally upon those whose marriages have failed? How we need to cleanse our own motives when seduced into judging others!

Having said all this, we are not for a moment suggesting that the demands of the Sermon on the Mount be relativized or compromised in any way. On the contrary, we take God's absolutes with utter seriousness. Can the Holy Spirit direct any Christian conscience to a less serious response? This, then, is the necessary backdrop against which we plead on behalf of those whose marriages have failed. Admit it—are we not all at times caught in tangled webs of our own making, sometimes finding them inextricable? Eventually, in the course of affairs, we know that a point of no return has been reached; the die is cast. There is nothing we can do to reverse the situation. And yet, through it all, the God of all grace has even then been devising solutions that will prove triumphant in the end. How can we praise Him enough that He sees the end from the beginning and moves toward that end through all the intervening circumstances! Incidentally, a marvelous study of this New Testament theme can be traced around the word *nevertheless*. This is what the Good News is all about—a "nevertheless" God!

It is not really that we want a license for complicity with the forces of marital destruction, as others may thoughtlessly accuse. We are simply and deeply concerned with the realities of life as they are and shall ever be. In loving-kindness beyond our imagination, God takes cognizance of our struggles, always making a counterprovision. His accommodation to these realities in the wonder of His grace is only temporary, since one day even this necessity will be banished forever. Meanwhile His ministry of grace is a constant reminder that what "is" ought "not to be." His grace must ever be seen against the backdrop of the divine "No!"

Martin Dibelius concluded his important study of the Sermon on the Mount by saying that Jesus proclaimed the pure will of God in an absolute way. At no time is God's will conditioned upon man's ability to respond. Neither is His absolute will validated only under future-kingdom conditions. The ultimate validation remains for the time of the fully consummated kingdom, but it is still God's moral imperative for His people now. In the prospect of the coming kingdom, Jesus proclaims God's moral demands without regard to present limitations. His absolute will is not dependent upon kingdom realization completely. It is eternal like Himself, and its imperatives apply to all men at all times. That the fulfillment of ethical absolutes is presently hampered by conditions of our existence in the world is seen by Dibelius as a sign of this passing age, harbinger of that to come. The negative, as a foil, illumines the positive!

But, for now, prior to the kingdom's establishment, our calling is to live out the moral imperatives so far as we are able, knowing the limitations imposed by human weakness and sin. Inasmuch as we have the Holy Spirit's enablement, we are responsible for personal failure. Our purpose, however, should never be to make provision for failure in advance, as though this were inevitable. Anticipation of failure is the first step in that direction. Instead, we are to commit ourselves without reservation to successfully living out His will. Only as we miss the blessing of God's primary plan do we need His intervention by grace. But every manifestation of God's renewing grace should humble us, motivate us to more consecrated living, and make us entirely dependent upon His resources for an increasing measure of victory.

By now it should be plain that we cannot dismiss the radicalized demands of the Sermon on the Mount as though somehow they do not apply to us in all their rigor. Rather, we seek to implement these moral imperatives in our daily lives for our own sake, still more for the glory of God. At the

same time, a consistent walk in His righteous ways is a
powerful protest against the fallen age. The reign of God becomes visible in our lives, showing forth something of the
powers of the age to come. In this way, we are signs of the
coming kingdom, signs that something marvelous has already begun in advance of that kingdom. Even temporary
defeats and failures take place within a larger context of ac-
cumulating victories. Something as devastating as, say,
an irreversible marriage failure (should it come to this) can
be transcended either by a God-honoring restoration or by a
God-honoring second marriage.

Is Cause the All-Important Factor?

Since justification of remarriage rests with the nature
of God's grace, ultimately it has nothing to do with either
innocence or guilt. Is this a surprising thought? Think
it through carefully, for it is crucial to understanding the
full nature of grace. For if grace is grace indeed—recall
our definition—it is not subject to preconditions. It is not
granted for reason of cause—any cause—nor is it denied for
reason of cause—any cause. Cause is not the all-important
factor we tend to make it. The debate over cause loses its
central relevance in light of what God's grace is all about.

If we think about this with any depth of perspective, we
see that Jesus was actually the only one who spoke to the
question of cause, doing so within the particular, limited
context of the Pharisees' question relating to Mosaic law.
Curiously, Paul did not address the question of cause directly at all. As close as he came was to answer the Corinthians' inquiry as to whether a Christian should divorce
a pagan spouse. In the last analysis, a failed marriage
is a failed marriage, whatever the cause (more correctly,
"causes"). In any failed marriage among Christians, the
covenant of unity and fidelity has in some sense been dis-
avowed. Whatever is responsible for bringing about this
marital break, the grace of God is needed. And God's grace
is available! The guilty and the innocent, if such can be dis-

criminated, equally have to apply to God's grace. Whether there has been deliberate sin, or simply failure to achieve what was sincerely desired, there is need for God's forgiving, renewing grace. And, we repeat, it is available!

James Bales points out that when remarriage is denied for the guilty party, that one is being asked to remain celibate for the remainder of life. What is this, he asks, but "doing penance"? Full forgiveness is precluded if such a prohibition is sustained. It is tantamount to saying that celibacy and continued singleness are the required payment for the sin of divorce. Since this does not amount to restitution—nothing is restored—it is nothing other than payment for sin. Yet, ironically, of no other sin we could mention do we hear of penance being required. Why? Because penance is not a biblical principle!

Protestant doctrine, faithful to God's Word, rejects all notion of penance since this adds something of merit to grace, and grace would no longer be grace. When God forgives, He removes all penalty and guilt. Whenever we require that a person not remarry, we are doing two things: exacting penalty and perpetuating guilt. Now, if the grace of God brings freedom from both penalty and guilt—and it does—then we must exercise the same grace, lest we become guilty of exacting what God Himself does not exact. I for one would fear to be in this position.

It is in this connection that I have found myself saying with chastened heart that I would rather err on the side of grace than on the side of inflexible law with its cruel sanctions and prohibitions. Every pastor who thinks this through faces the same choice. In the final analysis, you and I must choose which it will be—law or grace. And, my dear, hurting Christian friend, God invites you to receive His free, overflowing grace! It may be His good pleasure to restore a completely broken marriage, making it far more than it ever was before. Or if it is truly irreversible, He may be pleased, to grant you a loving, fulfilling remarriage. Of one thing you may be sure: He wants to give you the best gift of love—the very best gift!

It seems fitting to close this long and detailed study on a personal note. I can surmise that some readers are indeed Christian, divorced, and agonizing over the decision whether to remarry or not. Hope struggles against despair as the forces of prohibitive legalism bare their strong, intimidating arm. I have heard too often of the pressures exerted by pastors and seminar leaders. The anxiety of making your own decision independently of teachers you respect, but whose position you cannot follow, literally rips at your heart. At times it seems your whole world has come to an end. Well, listen to this final word.

Jesus described the signs that would herald "the end of the age," saying "All these are the beginning of birth pains" (Matt. 24:3–8, NIV). *End* of the age . . . *beginning* of birth pains? Colin Wood, fellow sufferer, who for quite different reasons witnessed the end of his world only to find God's restoring grace more than sufficient for a new life, said it so well: "In the kingdom of grace, the end is always the beginning." So, whatever that new beginning may be for you in God's loving purpose, may you discover it through His sure leading and enter in with the joy of a gracious Lord!

Appendix A

What About Romans 7:1–3?

Some who teach "no divorce, no remarriage, no exceptions" refer to Romans 7:1–3 to bolster their position. This appears legitimate until one examines the context and considers the limits within which Paul is teaching as well as his immediate purpose.

> Do you not know, brethren—for I am speaking to those who know the law—that the law is binding on a person only during his life? Thus a married woman is bound by law to her husband as long as he lives; but if her husband dies she is discharged from the law concerning the husband. Accordingly, she will be called an adulteress if she lives with another man while her husband is alive. But if her husband dies she is free from that law, and if she marries another man she is not an adulteress.

What is the subject here? Not marriage. It is the nature of the law. Marriage is brought in incidentally as an illustration. The theme is carried over from the previous chapter, where Paul taught that the death of Christ gives us deliverance from the law (see also 7:4). We are henceforth free from it. Here, by way of analogy, he calls attention to the general law of marriage, namely, that a woman is legally bound to her husband so long as he is alive. Paul concerns himself only with the basic law of marriage, not with possible exceptions through lawful divorce. Such considerations would have carried his argument in a confusing direction, and the whole theme would be unnecessarily complicated. Paul would have had to discuss the exception that Jesus allowed as well as his own exception, allowed in the case of an unbelieving partner. He does not do this, nor is there reason why he should.

Paul is demonstrating the legitimate place of law in the regulation of marriage—its binding nature. The illustration has to do with a woman married to a man, then becoming in the eyes of the law an adulteress by living with another man. There is nothing said about lawful divorce and remarriage, nothing about the exceptions taught by Jesus and by Paul himself.

An important parallel comes before us in the synoptic Gospels. In Mark and Luke the general law of marriage is stated with no mention of possible exceptions; the general law is the sole consideration. Although twice in Matthew an exception is stated, the reason is that Matthew is not teaching the general law of marriage but confronting the question as to what possible causes might legally justify the dissolution of marriage.

Archbishop R. C. Trench long ago set down the principle at work here: "Nothing is proved by the absence of a doctrine from one passage, which is clearly stated in others." Thus we conclude that Romans 7:1–3 contributes nothing to our examination of texts on divorce and remarriage since this is clearly not its subject.

Appendix B

The "No Divorce, No Remarriage, No Exception" Teaching

How is the exception clause explained by those who teach "no divorce, no remarriage, no exception"? In national seminars in recent years, two approaches have surfaced. These views have historic roots but are rather recently promulgated among evangelicals. To this author they seem biblically weak.

First, there are those who teach that the exception clause does not refer at all to Christians in this or any other era, but only to Jewish couples in the betrothal stage of Jewish marriage. From the Gospel of Matthew, the example is given of Joseph, who purposed to divorce Mary privately when he discovered she was pregnant and knew he had not been intimate with her. This is an example of a legitimate use of divorce in Jesus' time. Alfred Edersheim writes, "It should be noted that the writing of divorcement was also essential in the case of the breaking of betrothal vows. At betrothal the bridegroom, personally or by deputy, handed to the bride a piece of money or a letter, it being

211

expressly stated that the man thereby espoused the woman. From the moment of betrothal both parties were regarded and treated in law (as to inheritance, adultery, need of formal divorce) as if they had actually been married, except as regarded their living together. . . ."

Betrothal was a formal act in Israel that was not continued in the Christian church. What we modern Westerners understand as engagement is nothing at all like Jewish betrothal. In betrothal a woman became a man's legal wife. Mutual obligations of marriage were then in effect. But, during the period of betrothal, generally a year, sexual relations were not permitted. Any unfaithfulness on the wife's part was considered adultery and punishable as such. Provision was made for private divorce, and a bill of divorcement was required. Divorce in this instance did not dissolve a one-flesh union because there was as yet no sexual union to dissolve. The divorce merely dissolved the betrothal bond. This view of the exception assumes that divorce is possible only where it does not affect a one-flesh union. Hence the restriction to betrothal divorce.

To understand the exception clause as restricted to this special sense of betrothal unfaithfulness requires one to find some indication in the context that *porneia* was being interpreted in such a narrow, specialized fashion. There is no suggestion of this whatever. It is secondary at best.

Is it reasonable to suppose that the Pharisees were testing Jesus as to the valid cause(s) for divorce among the betrothed? Hardly. What possible reason would they have? There was no controversy about betrothal divorce that could be used to entrap Jesus—the Pharisees' single motivation for testing Him. This was not what they had in mind, nor was it what Jesus had in mind in response to them. Much of His reply was spent talking about what marriage involved, not what betrothal involved (note Matt. 19:4–7). Jesus said, among other things, "For your hardness of heart Moses allowed you to divorce your wives [not "your betrothed"] . . ." (v. 8). Then He added, "And I say to you: whoever divorces his wife [not "betrothed"] . . ." (v. 9). Had Jesus any thought of restricting His exception to those who were betrothed, no one would have guessed it. Furthermore, the Scripture at the center of Jesus' debate with the Pharisees was Genesis 2:24 and Deuteronomy 24:1–4. Neither of these Scriptures refer to betrothal, only to marriage. So this interpretation strains to find something other than the natural and expected meaning.

It would be difficult if not impossible to find unequivocal examples of *porneia* as denoting betrothal unchastity. William Heth and Gordon Wenham in their excellent study (*see* For Further Reading) conclude, "But the widespread testimony of the early Christian writers makes it less probable that the betrothal view can best account for the biblical and patristic evidence." We regard betrothal unchastity as one of the valid but secondary meanings of *porneia*—an inclusive term, as we are seeing.

A second interpretation of the exception clause that has captured the attention of some scholars is that Jesus is simply acknowledging the valid dissolution of illegitimate marriages, those that fall under the prohibited degrees of consanguinity and affinity as detailed in Leviticus 18:6–18. Jesus (or at least Matthew) is speaking to Jewish concerns only, to Jews under the law of Moses. In cases where Gentile converts are in marriages that fall under these prohibitions, while divorce generally is not allowed, the dissolution of such marriages makes up the exception. The exception would be Jesus' way of saying (as reported by Mark and Luke) that divorce is unallowable, "but of course I'm not including cases of illegitimate marriage."

It is true that there were illegitimate marriages that according to Mosaic law were to be terminated. There was consanguinous marriage, for example—marriage where the blood ties were too close and so forbidden. It is true that *porneia* was used in a secondary sense to refer to such marriages. But it was always the context that indicated such a meaning. In the discussion of Jesus with the Pharisees, there is no hint of any kind that this secondary reference might even possibly be in view. Had this been the case, so contrary would it be to natural expectation that an explanation would be called for. Jesus was perfectly aware of that. Again, there was nothing the Pharisees could find in the law relating to illegitimate marriages that could be used to put Jesus to the test, nothing to entrap Him or divide Him from the people. The Pharisees had no concern whatever for annulment cases. Here there was no divorce procedure because none was needed, and hence there was nothing to debate. Illegitimate marriages need only be witnessed to and declared so. As far as Jesus was concerned, in His part of the discussion He referred to wives but never once hinted that He meant "wives" in an illegitimate sense.

Now, of course, *porneia* could refer to sexual intercourse within the prohibited degrees mentioned in Leviticus 18:6–18; Acts 15:20, 29; and 1 Corinthians 5:1. But to restrict the meaning of *porneia* in Matthew to illegitimate marriages is clearly to go against the order of the argument, which is about marriage, not invalid unions. Jay Adams adroitly asks, "Why would Jesus gratuitously introduce a matter governed by entirely different Mosaic legislation, concerning which there was no controversy, and about which the Pharisees had no need for either reassurance or correction?"

Why *Porneia* Instead of *Moicheia*?

If Jesus meant adultery in the exceptive clause, why did He use *porneia* when the explicit word for adultery is *moicheia*? Would this not have saved a lot of misunderstanding and controversy, which Jesus Himself knew would arise? Well, for a rather obvious reason, really. *Porneia* is inclusive, so as to cover such wrong relationships as adultery, prostitution, consanguinous marriage, incestuous marriage, or homosexual marriage, for example. To have used *moicheia* would have construed a more restricted meaning than Jesus intended. In other words, there is merit in the supposition that although Jesus used *porneia* in the expected sense of adultery, He employed a concept broad enough to encompass illegitimate marriages, which carried the same guilt of unlawful sexual intercourse, unlawful cohabitation. This breadth of meaning is the most a careful scholar might allow, being scrupulous to keep the primary, expected meaning foremost. This is precisely why many versions translate "unchastity".

For Jews familiar with the Old Testament and other non-canonical writings, there was familiarity with Jeremiah 3, where in the Septuagint Greek version *porneia* is used to mean adultery. The word described faithless Israel, the wife of Yahweh. Israel's faithless consorting with the world is described in Ezekiel 16 as fornication *(porneia)* and later reaffirmed as fornication that is adultery *(moicheia)*. Further examples can be found in Hosea 3:1, 3 and Ecclesiasticus 23:23 in the Apocryphal writ-

ings. In another non-canonical writing, Sirach 23:22–23, the unfaithful wife is said to have "committed adultery by fornication."
By this seemingly strange use of the two terms, the intent is to
say that by sexual unfaithfulness she violated her covenant commitment to her husband.

We quickly concede that illegitimate marriage might, by extension, be included in what Jesus meant by *porneia*. We cannot
be confident of that, but we can be confident that this is not the
primary idea. Nor did Jesus slip in a secondary meaning to be
the whole meaning without telling the Pharisees that this was
what He was doing. We should remember, too, that teams of fine
scholars have been employed in making the various versions of
Scripture that enrich us today. The more familiar, accepted versions translate *porneia*, as we indicated in Chapter three, as
"fornication," "adultery," "sexual unfaithfulness," "unchastity."
They found no reason whatever to take a secondary meaning and
translate it "except for illegitimate marriages." It remains a
cause for curiosity why interpreters would go to such lengths to
avoid the primary and expected meaning unless it were to grasp
any possible reason to support their anti-divorce bias.

Why Are We Not Told About the Shammai-Hillel Controversy?

Why is it not explicitly said that the Pharisees were testing
Jesus in order to expose which side of the Shammai-Hillel controversy He would choose? Once more, the reason is rather obvious.
Since the Pharisees sought to entrap Jesus, they were clever
enough to try to avoid showing their hand. Why tip off Jesus to
their motive? They attempted to be as subtle as possible, never
mentioning the two rabbinical schools of thought, never bringing up the controversy that divided the people. They very well
may have hoped that Jesus was unaware of that division of opinion. They directly posed the question to Him that was central to
the debate. Then, if Jesus declared Himself on one side or the
other, they could accuse Him of taking sides. But why scare off
Jesus at the very start?

Jesus followed suit in His reply. Although perfectly aware that
they were seeking to pin Him to the wall, Jesus avoided any mention of the two debating schools. He played the game along with
them. In doing so, He had His own reasons. He was acting, not re-

acting. He spoke on His own authority. His teaching was far more fundamental and far-reaching, far more authoritative than anything relating to human schools of interpretation. He stood above them all. And what He did was to shift the emphasis away from the question of cause for divorce to the question of God's intent for marriage. He moved away from what is relative to what is absolute, from man's rules to God's ideal. He wanted them to see the perfect righteousness of the "no divorce, no remarriage, no exception" intention of God. Yet Jesus did not leave it at this; after all, He was dealing with real situations and with a controversy over cause for divorce. He did not brush aside the Mosaic provision, for Moses got his instruction from God. Thus, while Jesus reinforced the design of God that there be no divorce and remarriage according to absolute righteousness, He at the same time could say in practical terms, "Yes, the intrinsic bonding of marriage can be violated and broken; that violation is sexual unchastity."

Jesus nowhere said, "I agree with Shammai," although the two were essentially in agreement that sexual unfaithfulness was the cause that justified divorce. The Divine Teacher left it to the Pharisees to see that, if anything, it was Shammai who agreed with Jesus, not Jesus with Shammai. And Jesus was going beyond Shammai in His teaching about remarriage.

Anti-divorce teachers fly in the face of the vast numbers of scholars who have expertise in determining what *porneia* means in this context, context being all-important. Worse still, not to acknowledge to their constituencies that a majority of theologically sound biblical scholars are in disagreement with their teaching is both irresponsible and unethical. By the same reasoning, this author wants it to be plain to the reader that some of the directions of thought in this book contain recent thinking that differs from older, more traditional ethics. Thus, while this author's understanding of *porneia* is long-established in evangelical scholarship, the larger thesis of this book and its supporting evidence should be judged on the basis of how well it deals with Scripture, how theologically sound it comes across, and how nearly it represents the mind of Christ and the ruling ethic of the New Testament. It must also be judged on the basis of what competent critics say in their reviews. In other words, all sides must be scrupulously studied, especially by anyone who faces a personal decision or who is counseling others. One thing is certain, however; readers are entitled to read an in-depth study that is something besides a rehash of older, more entrenched views. We need not venerate the past to the point of being myopic about present thinking. It is my hope that readers will learn how to balance one-sided teaching—whichever side it may represent—watching always for inflexible dogmatists, and especially those who assume what they set out to prove. In this ongoing process may there be an increasing understanding of the compassionate God and the wonder of His mediating, renewing grace! There is no evangelical consensus on this subject today. May every serious endeavor lead us closer together!

Appendix C

What Serious Consequences?

In some circles where the "no divorce, no remarriage, no exception" position is taught, an additional element is added. It is that there are ten serious consequences for all those who remarry after divorce. Mind you, these are not the consequences of pain and devastation felt by many. Nor are they such consequences as loss of family or financial resources, alienation from in-laws, or the divided loyalties and ensuing confusion that afflict the children. All these and more are possible consequences that may occur in any given divorce situation. But what is being taught are consequences that God brings, the allegation that He can never bless a remarriage, that only severe judgment can come upon such a marriage. No consideration is given particular circumstances or conditions. There is just a blanket judgment. Thus a guilt trip is quite indiscriminately laid upon all who remarry after divorce. The questions we must ask are: Can these alleged consequences be established in Scripture? Are supporting passages directly related to the issue of divorce and remarriage, or are they contrived so as to apply? In other words, are these consequences simply the judgments of biased teachers?

219

I have consistently found that when supposedly supporting scriptural citations are examined, none of them directly bears on the subject of divorce and remarriage. Each represents a principle imported from elsewhere in Scripture, most often from the Old Testament, then interpreted completely out of context so as to apply. These are contrived applications, as is apparent to anyone who examines them closely.

Of the ten serious consequences popularly taught, we will take the first in the series as our opening example. This will serve to demonstrate the faulty methodology. Then we can look at a couple of further examples of what this teaching attempts to force into serving as divorce-remarriage deterrents.

It is taught, "You will break a sacred vow." This is true, since marriage vows are sacred and divorce breaks those vows. But then the inference is drawn that in consequence of breaking a vow a person cannot be blessed by God; one's life is thereby taken out of the blessing of God. For scriptural support, the following passages are cited: Ecclesiastes 5:4–6; Psalm 56:12; Proverbs 20:25; Malachi 2:13–16. Then—and here is the scriptural sledgehammer—from Numbers 30:3–4 is derived the dire consequence. Read the passage carefully for yourself; better still, read the entire chapter.

Notice that the vows have nothing to do with marriage and divorce. Surprised? What are these vows? They are vows of personal dedication to God (not to one another). Reason cannot be stretched far enough to find a valid application to divorce! Ironically, verse 9 tells of "a divorced woman" (yes, a divorced woman!) making a vow. It can hardly be missed that a divorced woman is appropriately making vows of dedication and service to God. To learn something further about the making of vows and to whom they are made, see Leviticus 27.

Now, the real question, of course, is this: Are Christians under the Mosaic law regarding vows? Clearly not. In fact, if Christians are under Mosaic law at all, they are under Deuteronomy 24:1–4, which permits divorce and remarriage! The whole case breaks down when we acknowledge that we are not under Mosaic law. The problem is one of misapplication of the Old Testament law.

Now, to be sure, it is a serious thing to make any kind of vow and break it, especially when God is called to be witness to that vow.

Just how are we to understand marriage vows? To whom are they made? They are made between husband and wife, not to God. He is called to be witness to those vows but is not the object of them. That He is called to be witness is recognition of God's sacred institution of marriage and the sacredness attached to a couple's making marriage vows. But those vows obligate a couple to fulfill duties to each other. These duties are to be in accord with the divine institution of marriage. The couple sincerely asks God to consecrate their marriage and give them the ability to make it what it should be.

To break these vows is to break them with the marriage partner. And, as with all human vows, individuals know that however sincerely the vows are made, however sacred they regard them at the time they are made, fulfilling them is necessarily provisional: "So far as we are able." Even the President of the United States, when sworn into office, places his hand upon a Bible and swears (vows) his acceptance of the duties of his office. But he adds, "So help me God," in recognition that by himself, apart from God's help, he may be unable to fulfill his vows. So it must ever be with marriage vows.

This important distinction between vows made to God and vows made to another individual is reflected in Jewish marriage. The Jewish term for marriage was *kiddushin,* which means "sanctification" or "consecration." This term means that something is totally set apart. In its highest usage it describes something dedicated to God as His exclusive possession. Anything totally surrendered to God is *kiddushin.* In marriage this does not mean two people are consecrated to God, but to each other. The one becomes the exclusive possession of the other, and vice versa—as much so as something consecrated to God becomes His absolute possession. This truth was implied in the Genesis account: that a husband would leave his father and his mother and cleave to his wife. It is also what God meant by their becoming "one flesh." But this is not the same as saying that the two are consecrated to God, and it is not what two people mean when they consecrate themselves to each other. They are asking God to consecrate their marriage—to set apart their marriage as a sacred union. Since this is never to be taken lightly, so far as possible this should serve as a deterrent to marriage dissolution.

Now, if despite every effort to keep their vows, marriage fails, a couple may have to acknowledge, "Yes, we desired to keep our vows to each other, and we were sincere in those vows. But we were unable to do so. We tried, but we failed."

There is, of course, a vast difference between deliberately breaking vows with little regard for their sacredness and simply seeing a vow broken because, in spite of everything, two people could not fulfill the conditions once thought possible. But it is faulty interpretation to infer that every divorcing couple across the board is under judgment as vow-breakers and shall suffer dire consequences as being outside the pale of God's blessing. It applies Old Testament Scripture where Old Testament Scripture does not apply! Worst of all, it implies that there can be no spiritual recovery except through marital reconciliation. This author has witnessed his share of lives devastated by this teaching. As many counselors have commented, how much better it is to train people to understand and sustain the goals of Christian marriage than to contrive threatening consequences in the attempt to ward off divorce.

Looking at the other so-called consequences taught by the popular anti-divorce school, one is impressed with how irrelevant or wrongly used are their scriptural supports. Strangely, these so-called consequences are given as a blanket judgment without regard to individual circumstances. There is no attempt to discriminate between cases. It is the old trick of universalizing from a few sample cases. The worst part of it is that nothing positive is offered hurting people who have struggled through an unwanted divorce—nothing but legalistic prohibitions. The only option offered by some anti-divorce teachers is "Suffer it for the Lord's sake." Pious as that may sound, we ask, "Is this really the best the Lord has for those who have suffered enough already, and perhaps against their will?" Is it God's will to cancel all possibilities for normalizing life once more, for restoring family life upon a strong marital basis? Something professional Christian counselors discover early in their practice is that not all personal and family values are necessarily kept intact when a couple decides to stay married despite enormous conflicts, nor are all personal and family values necessarily lost when a couple divorces. Some individuals suffer crippling consequences as a result of divorce; others are set free from destructive bondage. Some children are hurt when their parents divorce; other children are hurt when their parents stay together. The complexity and intensity of human relationships often tell the story. The teaching that contrives nothing but negative consequences, applying them to every divorced and remarried person, evidences a completely negative mind-set toward human relationships quite unknown to Scripture.

Another of the supposed ten serious consequences is worthy of attention, inasmuch as it has had a peculiarly devastating effect upon many sensitive people and has been widely discussed among professional Christian counselors to whom these people turn. The teaching is as follows: When a father or mother gets divorced and remarries, the message to their children is "Marriage is not a lifelong relationship. If your first marriage fails, no matter, you can always try again." The serious consequence attached to this: "You will lower God's standard for the children." Let us examine this.

The premise is that divorce-and-remarriage always and in every case is destructive to children and to the way they will value marriage as a result. Is this true? Not necessarily, and in some cases the very opposite occurs. From countless studies made by family experts, this is a faulty premise. A God-honoring remarriage where there is peace and united Christian parenting, which children did not experience in the previous marriage, may well teach them that marriage is not the horrible thing they were led to believe in the previous marriage. Here are partners who love each other, talk together a lot, enjoy common interests, find no reason to fight with each other. What we are saying is that the children have a new model, a positive Christian model. They now have an opportunity to see Christian family completeness that they in turn can emulate in their own adulthood. This is far superior to any single-parent model the anti-remarriage teacher might have encouraged. And, so far as the suggestion that an adequate model might be achieved by having a Christian man (someone else's husband) play a fatherly role in that single-parent home, I am afraid few counselors could buy that idea. For here is an unnatural, awkward relationship loaded with problems and possible temptations.

The anti-remarriage teaching argues that there is an advantage in being a single parent, inasmuch as—whatever happened in one's marriage—this can now be used to build Christian character qualities in one's life. What twisted thinking! This, again, hardly provides an adequate answer to basic human needs. First, it assumes that one must invariably live with "whatever

happened in your marriage," that change cannot take place. It
assumes that one is locked into an admittedly unhappy and un-
healthy status, having been left a single parent. Is not the real
answer much more humane, let alone Christian? On balance, is
it not more reasonable to believe that God calls *some* divorced to
remain single and others to remarry, and also that He can build
these Christian character qualities in either case? *The one significant factor is God's particular call.* To suggest that character
development is somehow restricted to those who remain single
following divorce is to fly in the face of reality and good sense.
God's maturing process is not restricted to any set of circumstances. Our God is greater than all circumstances!

This rather peculiar viewpoint being taught by the anti-
divorce school is further extended to teach that one should remain a single parent and go on to find one's special rewards in
God. Become content in Christ; let God become a father to your
children as well as protector to the woman. Psalm 68:5 is cited in
support of this notion.

Now, Psalm 68:5 simply refers to God as "Father of the father-
less and protector of widows." The psalmist is not talking about
the divorced. There is nothing whatever to suggest from this that
we are uniformly to disregard the reconstituting of family life. It
is simply and clearly a promise that God will not forsake the widowed or their children; He will be a protector and provider. "Widowed," not "divorced," are the subject of this text.

Contrary to these contrived judgments and consequences,
countless reconstructed families are living out harmonious and
godly lives, blessed in their life together and in their service for
the Lord as they make a positive Christian contribution to
their community.

These examples of the popular anti-divorce teaching in our
country should caution us to examine closely every rationale
given in support of a position that attempts to make the Bible a
code book replete with penalties and consequences for every supposedly wrong action. We should always ask for more than a
proof-text or two, especially when the proof-texts cited bear no
direct relation to the subject at hand. What does the Scripture
say within its context? What does it directly concern? Is the extended application a valid one?

While this writer finds nearly all these "serious consequences" in the popular literature of the anti-divorce seminars

to be merely contrivances without validity, a balancing word needs to be said about consequences in general. This is especially needful for any reader who may presently be planning divorce. For, despite every hope and precaution, this book doubtless will be read by some who are looking for justification for plans to leave a marriage. With twisted logic and self-delusion, they may rationalize as follows: "God is a God of love and grace, forgiving and offering a second chance. I can expect Him to look with grace upon me and forgive me, even though I'm determined to pursue this romantic interest that will destroy my marriage. In spite of my wrong intentions, God knows my weakness and will forgive me. I know He loves me and will want everything to work out well in the end."

Three things need to be said. First, this is twisted thinking, deceiving the person who is searching for any possible excuse to justify a wrong act. Second, we are all responsible for our choices, whether we choose what we know to be God's will or do not choose it. Third, there is no guarantee that God will want everything to work out well in the end in spite of a deliberate choice to do the wrong. Quite the contrary.

All actions have consequences, natural consequences which are built into the very action itself. Classic drama builds upon this reality. When we go against God's order, deliberately disobeying His known will, there are consequences that follow as surely as night follows day. *A God of grace does not cancel out these consequences, unless in His sovereign will He chooses to do so.* The presumption is against His intervention. He may not impose penalties, but as Geoffrey Bromiley says, the consequences are the penalties! By our actions, we choose the consequences that for us will be our penalties.

It is a serious thing to plan divorce in order to fulfill some selfish desire, to have one's own way, sinning against the marriage covenant. Later penitence may bring God's forgiving, healing touch, but life will have been strewn with asked-for consequences. God is not mocked! We cannot plan to break His will without consequences. It is this that we need to emphasize in our teaching. If we do, we shall not need to contrive false and unscriptural consequences. Nor will we suggest the same consequences as applicable to all remarrying people regardless of the reasons and circumstances of their status as divorced.

Appendix D

New Approach to Social Ethics

There are many modern helps in our understanding of biblical ethics today—and how much we need them as we face the complexity of contemporary social problems! Aids are found in the methods employed in other disciplines. Take the advanced "systems approach." Every system has its subsystems as well as interrelationships with yet other systems outside itself. The whole is seen as something greater than a collection of separate parts, more than what constitutes a single system. This same approach enables us to take a more sophisticated look at ethical situations and their special interrelationships. With this method we see the broader picture; we have an additional means for dealing with complex social issues heretofore undeveloped. Just as today we have social problems never before experienced or even foreseen by former generations, so we have means for applying scriptural principles formerly unexplored. While Scripture does not change, nor the moral principles embodied in Scripture, our ability to understand and make proper applications changes continually. We are constantly advancing in our ability to grasp the larger meanings of God's Word. The marvel of God's Word is that

227

it is formulated supernaturally so as to allow for taking such a systems approach, thereby finding new applications from within the very same pages that spoke to the different needs of former generations. Utilizing this method to pursue an understanding of divorce and remarriage is what this book is all about.

The tragedy that plagues a developmental approach to Scripture interpretation is that there are always those for whom any new approach, any new insights or methodologies, are greeted as heretical departures even before these methods are put to the test. Defensively postured Bible students fear that God's Word is being tampered with, not being allowed to say what it says. Yet this very fear has the effect of narrowing one's openness to what Scripture truly intends to say in the context of our times. Thus truth is shut off from those who most desire to remain faithful to biblical revelation. Worse still, it makes them hypercritical of equally earnest students who seek to be faithful to God's Word while searching out all possible applications to difficult modern problems, students willing to risk being innovative in their search. Nonetheless, we know that advanced insights do come to those who are willing to step out and use new methods for examining God's truth.

A point made early in this book is that both Jesus and Paul treat the question of divorce and remarriage within specific contexts, each with its own special features. They teach within situations and in answer to certain questions. This fact is crucial to our evaluating the biblical data base upon which we expect to arrive at an ethical judgment relevant and adequate to the divorce issue of our day.

With our proclivity for ready-made, universalized Bible solutions for all social problems, it is easy to ignore contexts and situations—the special features that bring out particularly appropriate teaching. We grasp at Bible statements. But to give little or no heed to the specific context is to make the Bible say either more than it intends—or less. We assume unwarranted generalizations where they are not intended, or we miss broad principles where they are.

Nothing today should be more apparent than that Jesus spoke to specific contexts, which in turn define the limits of proper application. Paul himself spoke within a particular context when he addressed certain divorce-and-remarriage questions raised by a particular Corinthian congregation. In this instance we must also attempt to know the proper limits of application. So we insist throughout this study that where Scripture is clearly given within specific contexts, we must interpret it contextually.

In Richard Longenecker's *New Testament Social Ethics for Today,* we are reminded that during the sixties and early seventies we rejected "contextualism" and "situation ethics" altogether, and for very good reasons. Quite correctly we rejected the view of such scholars as Joseph Fletcher and Paul Lehmann, who put ethics on a subjective rather than objective basis and in the process ruled out prescriptions and proscriptions of Scripture as moral norms. For these scholars, Jesus' declarations of kingdom righteousness no longer served as the sure basis for ethical decision making. Moral action is to be judged on a purely subjective scale. This requires a principle of action, of course, and the New Testament provides that principle—love. The sole standard for moral judgment becomes unconditional love; no other standard is needed. A popular form of the ethic in question ran something like this: "Is this action of mine the most loving response I can make in this particular situation?" If one could answer "Yes," then no further considerations entered in, since it simply involved what love would do in this situation. Situation ethics came into vogue.

In itself, of course, this is an appealing and quite appropriate ethical principle, not to mention a well-established New Testament standard for personal conduct. Who can fault the principle of love? Jesus said it summed up all the commandments. But was it meant to stand alone? Who decides what "love" is in a particular situation? What standard of loving are we to employ? How does love correlate with God's other attributes? That is, what other elements of God's character enter in? Where does God's sovereign purpose fit in? These and other questions soon made sole dependence upon "love" seem in the end a simplistic and totally inadequate approach to personal ethics. For evangelicals the matter was dead, buried, and forgotten.

But wait. We must ask in retrospect whether there was an element of truth that we too-quickly discarded. Did we throw the baby out with the bathwater? Did we distort the biblical position by overreacting? Longenecker says we did. Contextualism, he insists, is a necessary aspect of ethical judgment if we are to be truly biblical. Contextualism, he continues, assists us in our making adequate sense out of the data of life, data that is requisite to decision making. We are thus able to think and act rightly about God's revelation of His will for our current dilemmas. Contextualism, then, is clearly necessary to our grasping the parameters of an issue such as divorce and remarriage. It provides an important part of a complete approach, although only one part.

By way of example, Longenecker points to the composition of the four Gospels, reminding us that each writer adapted his presentation to the perspectives and concerns of his respective community. In consequence, each Gospel must be interpreted in terms of the writer's objectives. Not to do so is to miss the distinctive message of each. Equally risky is the possible misapplication of that message to ourselves. The writers, in other words, tailored their message to concrete situations, and this in turn must be adapted to the concrete situation in which we find ourselves. What we have, in short, is the principle of adaptation. But then is this not our normal expectation?

Longenecker further demonstrates that ethical issues in the New Testament are seldom presented in isolated propositions but more regularly appear in relational contexts. In this way guidelines are laid down to keep people's particular circumstances in view. This, too, is contextualism in its best sense. So, on balance, in ethical decision making we first take care to incorporate the statements of Scripture, both *pre* scriptive and *pro* scriptive alike; this is our revelational data base. Next we note any significant features that relate to specific contexts. Then we seek to discover the extent to which an ethical principle is meant to apply (or not apply) to other like situations within the general category of the problem being addressed. Of course, all along the way we seek the direct illumination of our understanding by the Holy Spirit. Our minds and spirits are a vital part of the process. And the question of our own growth and maturity enter in. As our own capacities grow, the Spirit of God leads us into new, more comprehensive understanding of scriptural truth and its application. We have an increasing ability to adapt moral principles to contemporary problems. This is a gift we may expect to develop within the church.

To anyone with eyes to see, the New Testament presents the developing efforts of the early church to take theological and ethical truths and work out the ramifications from what was still a rudimentary basis in faith. Taking a developmental approach to New Testament interpretation, we conclude that Scripture was not meant to be the final formulation of theology and ethics, but rather the authoritative revelational base upon which developments of theology and ethics subsequently build. As the authoritative Word of God, it is altogether adequate to this task of building systems of thought. Thus we have an important body of biblical literature we call "theological ethics." Of course, theologies and ethical systems are not themselves the Word of God, so they must be held tentatively, always subject to review and correction. In this category we must place the developing thought of this book; it, too, must be held tentatively, subject to review and correction as our biblical understanding expands. The church, under the ministry of the Spirit, has a self-correcting capability, so we should not fear striking out into new fields of biblical examination. Earnest attempts at new understanding are not to be condemned, as though there were something inherently evil about progress in thought. Rather, the freedom to explore, examine, and express new insights requires only a correlative freedom to criticize and correct what the larger body of biblical scholars find questionable or wrong. This author would want his work to be subject to this ongoing critical process. For now, here is some biblical thinking to stretch your mind and invite a personal response.

For Further Reading

Cerling, Charles. *The Divorced Christian*. Grand Rapids: Baker, 1984.

Hosier, Helen K. *To Love Again: Remarriage For the Christian*. Nashville: Abingdon Press, 1985.

Richards, Lawrence. *Remarriage, A Healing Gift From God*. Waco: Word, 1981.

Small, Dwight. *How Should I Love You?* San Francisco: Harper and Row, 1979.

_____ *Marriage as Equal Partnership*. Old Tappan, N.J.: Revell, 1980.

_____ *Your Marriage Is God's Affair*. Old Tappan, N.J.: Revell, 1979.

Smedes, Lewis B. *Love Within Limits: A Realist's View of I Corinthians 13*. Grand Rapids: Eerdmans, 1978.

Smoke, James. *Living Beyond Divorce*. Eugene, Oreg.: Harvest House, 1985.

Note: The anti-divorce school of teaching is associated popularly with such names as Bill Gothard, Charles Ryrie, Carl Laney, less popularly with Abel Isaksson, Jacques Dupont, William Heth, Gordon Wenham and others. Those who desire to study the scholarly work underpinning this school are directed to *Jesus and Divorce* by William A. Heth and Gordon J. Wenham (Thomas Nelson, 1984). Exegetical work and references are superior. The anti-divorce school is fragmented by a diversity of scriptural interpretations. There is no evangelical consensus today. We need opposing studies to sharpen and expand our thinking. This book is highly recommended.